The Old Gospel for the New Age

And Other Sermons

BY
PROF. H. C. G. MOULE, D.D.
*Norrisian Professor of Divinity; author of "Secret Prayer,"
"Commentary on Romans," etc.*

Wipf & Stock
PUBLISHERS
Eugene, Oregon

Wipf and Stock Publishers
199 W 8th Ave, Suite 3
Eugene, OR 97401

The Old Gospel for the New Age
and other sermons
By Moule, Handley C.G.
ISBN 13: 978-1-55635-458-8
ISBN 10: 1-55635-458-4
Publication date 5/1/2007
Previously published by Fleming H. Revell, 1901

TO THE REVEREND
CHARLES ARMSTRONG FOX
INCUMBENT OF EATON CHAPEL, LONDON.

Friend in the Lord, thy voice has lifted oft
My listening soul on paths of light aloft,
In church, in chamber, or where thousands met
In that white tent by Derwent's margin set.
Now for thy lot awhile thy God ordains
Silence, and shadow'd sight, and burthening pains;
In brief, a cross of crosses; yet (so fine
His art to use e'en ill to ends divine)
Ne'er to my spirit's ear and inward sense
Spoke clearer out in thee His eloquence.

PREFATORY NOTE.

THE following Sermons, it will be seen, were preached in several different pulpits. They range in time over several years. These circumstances will account for certain repetitions, here and there, of theme and thought, repetitions which might have been removed by rewriting before publication. But it seemed better to leave them as they stood, for the topics which have been thus touched and retouched are of an importance (whatever view is taken of them) which justifies reiteration.

May the true "Master of Assemblies" be pleased to use for His glory whatever in this little volume is of His truth.

CAMBRIDGE, *Easter*, 1900.

CONTENTS.

CHAPTER		PAGE
I.	THE OLD GOSPEL FOR THE NEW AGE	11

'He said unto them, Thus it is written, and thus it behoved Christ to suffer, and to rise from the dead the third day; and that repentance and remission of sins should be preached in His name among all nations, beginning at Jerusalem.'—LUKE xxiv. 46, 47.

II.	THE SECRET OF THE PRESENCE	31

'Thou shalt hide them in the secret of Thy Presence.'—Ps. xxxi. 20.

III	THE BRIGHT AND MORNING STAR	48

'I am the bright and morning Star.'—REV. xxii. 16.

IV.	SELF-SURRENDER AND ITS POSSESSIONS—I.	64

'Ye are not your own.—1 COR. vi. 19.
'All things are yours.'—1 COR. iii. 21.

V.	SELF-SURRENDER AND ITS POSSESSIONS—II.	79

'Ye are not your own.'—1 COR. vi. 19.
'All things are yours.'—1 COR. iii. 21.

VI.	THE SELF-CONSECRATION OF THE CHRIST	95

'Then said He, Lo, I have come to do Thy will, O God.'—HEB. x. 9.
'Then said I, Lo, I have come! I delight to do Thy will.'—Ps. xl. 7, 8.

VII.	THE INDIVIDUAL AND GOD	113

'But it is good for me to draw near to God.'—Ps. lxxiii. 28.

CONTENTS.

CHAPTER		PAGE
VIII.	Two Cambridge Saints: Nicholas Ridley, Henry Martyn	130

'Whose faith follow, considering the end of their conversation.'—HEB. xiii. 7.

| IX. | The Sight of Self and the Sight of Christ | 147 |

'When I saw Him, I fell at his feet as dead. And He laid His right hand upon me, saying unto me, Fear not; I am the First and the Last: I am He that liveth, and was dead; and, behold, I am alive for evermore, Amen; and have the keys of hell and of death.'—REV. i. 17, 18.

| X. | 'Lovest Thou Me?' | 164 |

'Jesus saith to Simon Peter, Lovest thou Me?'— JOHN xxi. 15-17.

| XI. | The Holy Spirit and the Love of God | 176 |

'The Love of God is shed abroad in our hearts, by the Holy Ghost which is given unto us.'— ROM. v. 5.

| XII. | The Angel's Visit | 188 |

'I am Gabriel, that stand in the presence of God, and I am sent to speak unto thee.'—LUKE i. 19.

| XIII. | The Ministry of the New Covenant | 201 |

'Who also hath made us able ministers of the New Covenant.'—2 COR. iii. 6.

| XIV. | The Lord's Brother: the Son of God | 216 |

'I saw James, the Lord's brother. It pleased God to reveal His Son in me.'—GAL. i. 19; 15, 16.

| XV. | Living Stones | 224 |

'Ye also, as living stones.'—1 PET. ii. 5.

| XVI. | Heart Purity | 232 |

'Blessed are the pure in heart.'—MATT. v. 8.

PROFESSOR MOULE.

BY W. ROBERTSON NICOLL.

DR. MOULE is the most influential member of the Evangelical party in the Church of England, but he is besides a teacher of all the churches. Dr. Dale, towards the end of his life, in a letter to his friend, Mrs. Richard Davies, of Treborth, wrote: "Mrs. Dale and I are venturing to send you Moule on the Romans. I am reading it with great interest, and I trust with profit. I do not always agree with him, but he has a deep knowledge of the things of Christ, and there is something contagious in his earnestness. His theology will, I suppose, recall to you the theology of your own earlier years." It is as a devout and learned theologian that he is generally known. He has been, and continues to be, a leader of what is known as the Keswick School. But Dr. Moule is a many-sided man, with wide interests in literature and in life. While tenacious of everything that is vital in the old Evangelical theology, he has a breadth of culture and sympathy which outsiders scarcely understand. His career at Cambridge was exceptionally distinguished. He was Second Classic in the Tripos of 1864, Browne's Classical Medalist in 1863, Fellow of Trinity from 1865-81, and Dean from 1873-6, and for two years, 1865-7, Assistant Master at Marlborough. He is not only a scholar, but a true poet. I do not say that this is proved by the fact that he gained the Seatonian Prize at Cambridge six times, but the first thing I ever saw from his pen was a little volume of verses which he has not included among the list of his works, but which contained some true and tender poetry, while the first thing he ever published (in 1865) was "Apollo at Pheræ: a Drama on the Greek Model." Even from his writings one might gather that he has a keen sense of humor; and he is, so far as I know, the only Evangelical in the Church of England at present who is a master of English style. Some of his finest passages might be set alongside of Dean Church's, and bear the comparison well. While he has not spared himself in work primarily devoted to the edification of Christians generally, he has found time to show himself a master in the art of exposition. His commentaries on the Pauline Epistles rank with the best. Dr. Moule, however, is even more of a theologian than of an expositor. He has a perfect mastery of the great Evangelical system, and knows how to keep dogma in constant connection with living Christian experience. Nothing so good of its kind as his small but packed "Outlines of Christian Doctrine" has been done since Amesius published his golden *Medulla*. To hear Dr. Moule one might be inclined to think that by temperament his piety would be a form of quietism; and certainly an element of quietism is not absent from his writing. But neither is it absent from the New Testament. I heard him once pray for the coming of the Kingdom, for the deliverance of the Church from the dangers that threatened her. He went on, "but let us not be anxious even about this."

Dr. Moule was born at Dorchester in 1841, the youngest son of the Rev. H. Moule, M. A., Vicar of Fordington. His family is still represented in the district, where a visitor will hear much of the living and of the dead. Into such particulars, however, I do not propose to enter. Dorchester has been made famous in English literature by Thomas Hardy and William Barnes, and both of these came into close connection with the Moule family. I remember first hearing of Fordington when visiting the venerable poet William Barnes at Came Rectory, Dorsetshire, more than twenty years ago. Mr. Moule regarded, and regards, his father and mother with peculiar reverence, and all through his writings there are allusions— sometimes direct, sometimes indirect—to the happy and the holy home where his youth was spent, and where he received the convictions to which he has never been false. One of his most beautiful poems was written in 1878, in Fordington

Church, where Dr. Moule was baptized, and where he first ministered as his father's curate:

> "Holy scene, and dear as holy,
> Let me ponder thee this hour,
> Not in aimless melancholy,
> But in quest of Heaven-given power:
> Seeking here to win anew
> Contrite love and purpose true;
> Near the Font whose dew-drops cold
> Fell upon my brow of old;
> Near the well-remember'd seat
> Set beside my mother's feet;
> Near the Table where I bent
> At that earliest Sacrament.
>
> Let me, through this narrow door,
> Climb the Pulpit's steps once more.
> Blessed place! the Master's Word,
> Child and man, I hence have heard;
> Awful place! for hence, in turn,
> I have taught, so slow to learn."

In his admirable little work on the "Evangelical School in the Church of England," just published by Messrs. Nisbet, he says, speaking of the Simeonite School, "My dear father (1801-80), if I may be pardoned another personal allusion to a memory evermore sacred to me, was a type of that noble generation. In his early manhood in charge of a large country parish, he procured a confirmation visit from Bishop Burgess of Salisbury; the old man cheered the younger in his unassisted efforts after thorough parochial care, saying how he found everywhere that men of his opinions were the active promoters of schools and diligent teachers of the young for confirmation. Meanwhile men of these opinions were called, like their leader at Cambridge, to not a little trial in the way of social exile. The story is well known of the lady who could not be driven in the Bishop of London's carriage to John

Venn's rectory at Clapham; it would compromise the Bishop; she must be set down a little way off, at a tavern, where Venn's two sons went to meet her. In 1829 a young clergyman came to begin work in his Dorsetshire parish. His neighbors were not particularly sociable; and he learnt through a friend, after a time, that at a meet of the hounds he had been discussed, and pronounced a 'Methodist,' on whom it was not necessary to call. But no one of that sort, so far as I have heard, ever thought of airing such troubles as a grievance; they came in the day's work for God." Not that Mr. Moule was without congenial clerical neighbors. His son says: "I should like to linger over the recollection, ever brighter and dearer to me, of a typical circle of the older Evangelical clergy, the former members of the Dorset Clerical Meetings, men like Henry Walter, Charles Bridges, Carr John Glyn, Reginald Smith, C. W. Bingham, Augustus Handley, Edward Stuart, T. W. Berridge, David Hogarth, a group whose manly, cultured, unworldly lives and firm enlightened faith presented a spiritual and social phenomenon which it would be difficult to surpass in its kind." It is worth recalling that Charles Bridges, of whom Dr. Moule says that the remembrance of him "shines on me like a ray reflected from the Chief Shepherd's face," died at Hinton Martell, in Dorset, in 1869. The one objection I should take to Dr. Moule's little book on the Evangelical School is that he does not sufficiently recognize the immense influence of Edward Bickersteth, whose books used to be found in the manses of Evangelical ministers all over Scotland.

Dr. Moule's life work has been done as a teacher of theological students. He was the first Principal of Ridley Hall, Cambridge, and occupied the position from 1881 to 1899. He raised it to a position of high influence as the most important institution of its kind. Now he has quitted it for the Norrisian Professorship of Divinity in the University of Cambridge. There is every reason to expect that Dr. Moule will now give the Evangelical party what it so much wants, an authoritative and up-to-date exposition of its doctrines. He is understood to be preparing a commentary on the Articles. Of

PROFESSOR MOULE.   9

Dr. Moule as a teacher of theological students one might say much, but it will be best to refer to his altogether charming book entitled "To my Younger Brethren," the chapter on Pastoral Life and Work. There the heart of the man is revealed. No one will be surprised to find that he puts in the forefront as a condition of ministerial efficiency, the secret walk with God, prayer, and the study of the Bible. Andrew Bonar tells us that in his busy life he endeavored to keep two hours every day for actual prayer, and still was unsatisfied. He said, "I can do more by praying than I can do in any other way." In connection with this Dr. Moule lays great stress on the study of the Bible itself. He urges that the Bible should be read at whatever cost of other religious reading. It is a very common thing to substitute practically for the Bible a little library—*livres de piété*, as the French would call them, small good books. To the Higher Criticism as such he has no objection. "The most earnest defender of the supernatural character of the Scriptures may be, and very often is, as diligent a higher critic as the extremest anti-supernaturalist." But he is very much disinclined to accept many of the results of criticism, opposing to them the testimony of Christ. Dr. Moule frankly deals with the clergyman's relation to women, warning curates against flirtation on the ground that if attentions go beyond a certain line, while nothing but courtesy is meant, a woman's life may be spoiled. He even urges his men not lightly to seek marriage, not lightly to make engagements even where they have a good assurance that all will be spiritually well, if there is a real probability of a married life clogged with pecuniary perplexities. He thinks that there are branches of ministerial work where a single man makes the better minister, and says that no true servant of God will allow himself to think first of an opening for marriage and then of an opening for ministry. In speaking of the preparation of sermons Dr. Moule is singularly silent about books. He says almost nothing as to the general culture of the preacher and the special culture, but he is quite clear as to the necessity for good style. "A neat, straight, well-worded sentence is not a mere literary luxury; it is a practical power.

It is far easier to listen to than a careless, formless sentence is, and is far easier to remember." He commends Mr. Spurgeon's style as more perfectly suited for every-day audiences, and says that he happens to know that Mr. Spurgeon always took great and systematic pains with his English. Dr. Moule advocates a simple, natural, and luminous division of sermons.

It need hardly be added that the spirit in which this great Churchman refers to other communions is invariably large and charitable. Few men know more of the eminent Christian teachers outside the Church of England, and he delights to know that, "as regards the Scottish and Continental Churches, it is not too much to say that, with the very rarest exceptions, English Church writers *of all schools* regarded them as sister Churches of the Reformation *till about* 1830."

I.

THE OLD GOSPEL FOR THE NEW AGE

Preached in St. Bride's Church, Fleet Street, at the Ninety-ninth Anniversary of the Church Missionary Society, May 2, 1898.

"He said unto them, Thus it is written, and thus it behoved Christ to suffer, and to rise from the dead the third day; and that repentance and remission of sins should be preached in His name among all nations, beginning at Jerusalem."—LUKE xxiv. 46, 47.

THE preacher called to minister to you to-night must needs feel his heart full of the future. He is indeed conscious also of the past—a wonderful past, a nearly finished century of grace and mercy, and of the patience and faith of saints. How can he not be stirred by the thought of those first days of our Church Missionary annals, those original acts of simple but supernatural obedience and reliance? An unpraised, unheeded group of pious men, our founders met to pray and to confer; they looked out from a threatened England upon a world at war, and they embraced the obligation to attempt from England the evangelization of the world! So began the story so familiar to us, and so dear, and which inevitably, by laws of human imagination, claims a peculiar realization as the landmark of a hundred years aproaches. It is a retrospect vastly various under all its unity—a long succession of suspenses, of fluctuations, of glowing hopes, of heart-sickening disappointments, of magnificent renewals of zeal, expectation, and advance. The first appeals to a Church almost more skeptical than indifferent; the slow growth of recognition and support; the first sacrifices and triumphs, in Western Africa, in New Zealand, in India and Ceylon, in Abyssinia, among the northern Redmen; the shocks and sorrows of the Niger Expedition, of the Sepoy Mutiny, of the wars and rebellion of China, of the wreck of the Maori race and Church—yes, and of many a crisis of discouragement at home: such are some of the features of our backward view. Then, nearer to us in time, we behold an ever-opening India, and wide doors unbarred on a sudden in Japan, and the long cloud of mystery swept from Eastern Africa, and North-Western America silently transformed into a province of missionary bishoprics. Then Hannington dies at the gate of Uganda, and the "Cambridge seven" make London and England listen as never before to the missionary call. A new departure is manifestly taken. It is a new era in point of zeal and purpose and provision of resources and offers of service and organizaton of prayer and labor.

The believing Church among us betrays now a consciousness larger and fuller than before that her light is given her that she may shine; she exists to be her Lord's implement for the evangelization of the world.

So our yesterday is strong in us, in this place of many memories, at this solemn date of period and reflection. Yet the future, immortal child of the immortal past, its effect and sequel, its longed-for flower and fruit, is present here in even greater power. We are met not for reverie half so much as for resolutions and advance. The names of our blessed fathers are dear to us, with an indescribable sense of loyalty and honor; but we cherish that sense not that we may build their cenotaphs, but that we may carry on their work. Our Jubilee is a commemoration, but it is much more besides; it is a summons afresh to the foot of the atoning Cross, and a new proclamation there of the power and liberty of the Spirit, that we may go out in it before our Lord to announce Him, the Liberator, to the world. Our centenary year is a point of sight for a wider landscape; but not only that we may review and estimate achievements: much rather we are looking forward, so far as mortal eyes can, into our second century, and the twentieth of our Lord. We want to see something, through whatever haze, of the vastness of the land in front, and how He would have us enter in, and set our feet here, there, and everywhere upon it, claiming it for Him.

I am only giving voice to all your hearts. In the three years' preparation for our Centenary nothing has been more prominent than the consciousness of the overwhelming claims of the future. In every possible way the Society has emphasized its resolve (to an extent I had almost dared to call excessive) to silence all congratulations, under the conviction that the work is only at its threshold, and encumbered even there with incalculable arrears. It has spoken as if there were little to utter, if anything, save humiliation for the past, and penitent purposes for the future: *Nil actum reputans, dum quid superesset agendum.* And the "agendum" is vast, and the night is coming down upon it, when no man can work!

To be sure, the non-Christian world has been lately traversed for the Gospel as never before. Three main masses of inhabited territory alone now remain practically untouched—Arabia, Thibet, with Nepaul on its southern side, and the great Soudan. But the penetration of the world in its breadth has only made us the more conscious of its depths. The millions of the unevangelized earth have, as it were, multiplied themselves before us, for we can count them better, and we can realize them better, too, in their greatness and in their need. Along with the stronger consciousness of their claim upon us for evangelization there grows the consciousness that the evangelization of such populations, and under such conditions, is no matter for forced marches, hurried inroads or feeble occupations. It calls for promptitude indeed, in the name of God. But it calls for patience and for thoroughness as well. In brief, it sets before the believing Church a task scarcely apprehended hitherto in its true proportions. It is a task which fills the whole immediate future with its greatness and variety, with its awfulness and its hopes; an enterprise compassable indeed in Christ, but only compassable by a Church altogether wakeful, "pressing towards the mark, forgetting the things which are behind, and reaching forth to those things which are before."

This deepening, gathering sense of the missionary future embodies itself around us in many methods and movements full of a new age. Within our Society I need but name the still young and growing work of the Gleaners' Union, with its fine simplicity of plan, its ubiquitous extension, its living network of contact and sympathy and its rich results. Quite outside our organization, yet touching and touched by it at innumerable points, lies the large sphere of spiritual influence whose center, in a certain sense, is the tent at Keswick. From that center to a memorable extent, notably within the last ten years, the misionary impulse has powerfully vibrated in (I venture to say) all the Reformed Churches, and most of all, if I read the facts aright, within our own. In no slight connection with this movement, while going upon a perfectly independent line, the Student Volunteer Missionary Union makes a sign and landmark of the times. It is the spontaneous issue of a deep loyalty to the Lord in our young educated Christendom, and as such it is an omen full of the future and of a glorious hope.

Its now well-known Watchword is a call energetically forward—"The evangelization of the World within this generation." In no uninformed or unconsidering spirit that watchword is explained by its responsible advocates. They do not mean an undisciplined enthusiasm, nor the least tinge of weak depreciation of long-tried methods and the glorious veterans of the field. They mean no blind and narrow indifference to the immovable claims of the work of God at home, where never was the call so acute, so intense, so awful as now, not for *any* laborers, but for laborers true to the heavenly Word and filled with the Holy Spirit of God. They avoid with growing care a certain tone of chiding—I had almost said of scolding—into missionary zeal, which has sometimes marred earnest appeals, striking a harsh discord with the blessed purpose of them. They are, as I believe, aware of the grave spiritual risks of an undue and premature *pressure* upon young men and women to sign declarations and promises. They know the need of waiting first for full light upon the conditions of the work, upon the whole range of personal duties, and upon God's whole purpose for the individual as shown in the build of character and faculty; woeful have been the mistakes sometimes made under oblivion of that need. But what these youthful servants of God do mean is a deliberate and believing "new departure" in the study of the vast non-Christian world as it is; and so, in the realization of its tremendous need, and so, in the response of the Church to the call of the Redeemer, "Whom shall we send, and who will go for us?" The blessing of the Almighty, in His grace and guidance, be upon them!

So to the future tend all our hearts. These recent drifts and currents of enterprise and aspiration all betoken a great passage forward, a period already upon us of large developments and marked transitions, the free recognition of new conditions, and the application to them of methods often new and always ready for modification. True, this last great

Students' Movement has wisely and rightly disclaimed all idle love of revolution for its own sake; in particular it has affirmed a full belief in the high value of educational and of medical missions, methods which have been sometimes assailed by a short-sighted criticism. More, I think, rather than less, as time rolls, and thought as well as faith develops, the movement shows its true cohesion with the past. But its gaze is on the future; it sets its feet, it stretches out its hands, towards the time that is to be, the things that are before. It appeals to the Church to be ready for many a bold advance of thought and of action in view of new regions, new problems of races and of faiths, new conditions of both the world and the Church, in an age when great chapters of history are written before our eyes within the limits of a month.

Let us be ready, in our Master's name, for the future, for the new.

But now I call you to a line of recollection drawn just the other way, yet in strong connection with this curve of change. Amidst all conceivable other alterations there is that which must be unalterable to the end. Our beloved Society may, and must, keep its mind open to all the counsels which its Lord may give it through His providence. It must be prepared, if the need should arise (I do not say it will), to deal in courageous independence with many a long tradition of method. But the supreme question after all is not of method, but of Message. And the Message, in its sacred essence, is of "the things which are, and are to come." In the twentieth century as in the nineteenth, in our second age as in our first, the Gospel of the grace of God, the Truth of sin and of salvation, the Word of the Cross of our Lord Jesus Christ, lives and abides for ever. It knows, likes its Source, no variableness nor shadow of turning; to-day and to-morrow it is the same.

This is a movement at which such a reminder is not out of season. At a time pregnant of change and transition in many things it is easy to get an impression that there must be change in all things. And beyond doubt the thought of modifications of the Christian Message has made itself abundantly felt, and felt in the most various quarters, in our day. There are advocates in numbers around us who would altogether difference what they mean by religion from what they mean by theology; we are to hold the one off as free as possible from the other. Perhaps it is the theology of the Evangelical Revival; perhaps it is the theology of the Reformation, true ancestor of the other, and itself the genuine heir, not only of the first days of the Faith, but of all

that was noblest in the medieval schools as well; perhaps it is the theology of St. Paul. Yes, we are not to be too submissive now even before an Apostle, even before the Vessel of election, chosen to bear the Name before the nations and before Israel.*
Religion is to be disengaged from too close a cohesion here. The warm messages of goodwill, of brotherhood, of altruistic sacrifice, of instincts for the unseen and the ideal, are not to be always encumbered with the dogmatic chain of guilt and judgment and expiation and faith and a mystic new creation. We are even to beware of too strait and exclusive a limitation within the lines of a Nicene account of the person of the Man of Nazareth. Many have been the manifestations of the Eternal and the Good. Does not the Bible itself speak of sundry times and divers manners? The mercy of God is indeed in Christ; but is it in Christ alone? Revere His character, carry out as far as you may His precepts, imbibe His spirit; but beware of too positive a theology of His origin and His being!

Other voices speak from a place far, far nearer the center of the Gospel, yet in a tone, I dare to say, never quite in concord with the full chorus of the Apostles. We are counseled by some Christians, perhaps, to remember the many-sidedness of the

* Acts ix. 15.

Gospel. It was given by its Lord for many ages and for many races. It must be expected, in its revolution upon its axis, to turn to this age, and to that, another face than that which their forerunners saw. It will be found to present to one race another range of its truths than that which regenerated a human family lodged upon another hemisphere. We are to beware of making always one doctrine the central and the radiating point. Or, again, if we do so, we are to see that we centralize *that* truth which alone can give significance to all the rest, and in which lies already hidden all the glory, the hope, the transfigured future, of man—the Incarnation of the Eternal Word. To certain times, to certain regions, another center, or what may have seemed such, may have been fitly presented; but for the world this was provisional. Atoning Sacrifice is great, but Incarnation is greater. What truth, what range of truth, can appeal as this can appeal to universal man, as it ascends in its majesty before him, and he recognizes in its mysterious splendor not only what God is, but what *he* is, what Man is, that God is mindful of him?

I do not think that I have misrepresented what seems to me a powerful and prevalent element in large regions of Christian thought around us, and God forbid I should forget the strong relation of that element to unmistakable and all-important data of the Scriptures. The Incarnation—it is indeed, from one great view-point, the fact of facts, the royal, the imperial glory of all truth and of all spiritual joy. None but the Incarnate Lord of the Scriptures and of the Creeds could be to us the Eternal Word from the Eternal Heart, and could bear away from us the immeasurable burthen which in the Fall we had dragged down upon ourselves. "When Thou tookest upon Thee Man, to deliver, Thou didst not abhor the Virgin's womb." "The Effulgence from the Father's Glory, the Expression of His Being, He took part in flesh and blood, and by Himself purged our sins, and sate down"—who but the Incarnate could so labor, and then so rest? —"on the right hand of the Majesty on high."*

But this truth of all truths becomes another thing when it is taken apart from its primary revealed occasion and purpose for our race. And what I humbly contend is that it is so taken when Christian thought treats it as a Gospel in and by itself. It is so taken when we presume to answer in the affirmative the unanswerable question (unanswerable, because Revelation is absolutely silent here, and speculation is out of all its rights): Would Incarnation have taken place, if man had never sinned? It

* Heb. i. 3.

is so taken from its true use in general when we attempt to present an *Evangelium* to any race, in any stage of development, in any tract of time, which does not put into the foreground man's sin, in its guilt (be this well remembered) as well as in its power, and "the redemption that is in Christ Jesus" in all its bleeding glory, the atoning work of Golgotha, the Sin-bearer for the condemned, the Head on which was laid the iniquity of us all, the Propitiation for our sins, without whose blood-shedding is no remission, but "in whom we have redemption through His blood, even the remission of our sins."

Yes, as we prepare to travel into another century, on our way to meet the Redeemer at His Coming, this, and nothing other nor less than this, must be the unfaltering watchword of our work and witness. "God forbid that we should glory," in any climate, amidst the listeners of any race, "save in the Cross of our Lord Jesus Christ"; in that ancient and wonderful meaning of those words, in which they connote the sinner's guilt, the satisfaction of his Redeemer, our healing by His stripes, our rest because of His agonies, our welcome because of His dark deserted hour, our justification by His being "made for us a curse," our life, our eternal life, because of the unique and awful glory of His most precious Death.

Immeasurably more things than this central splendor are contained in the Gospel of the Grace of God. All the antecedent and unbought love of the Eternal is in it; "for God so loved the world that He gave His Only Begotten." All the living glory of the work of the Eternal Spirit is in it; for "Christ redeemed us from the curse of the law, that we might receive the promise of the Spirit, through faith," and might, by that Spirit, in His power and fulness, experience a rest, and liberty, and purity, and joy, and everlasting hope, which is heaven itself begun upon the earth. In that Gospel—that revelation of Him "who loved us, and gave Himself for us," "who died for us and rose again"—lie at once the law and the motive force of a sacrifice of self for others which walks in simplicity and peace upon heights which alien philosophies and other Gospels attempt in vain effectually to climb. In it lie suggestions of promise, of deliverance, of blessing, vast as the universe of creation; "the creation itself shall be emancipated into the liberty of the glory of the sons of God."* But, *for us sinners,* these truths all roll their golden circles round the sun of the Atonement. The "innumerable benefits" are all grouped within the blood-besprinkled precinct of the Passion. Without Christ, who died for our sins, and, having

* Rom. viii. 21.

died, is risen again, faith has no foothold, and conscience no rest, and hope no eastern window, and man knows neither himself nor God.

Once more, I dare to affirm it, not only here and there, and at times, but at all times and in all places, this is the Gospel. It is this, it is this alone, which carries with it those two contrasted yet profoundly connected notes, that man is tempted to be ashamed of it, and that to believing man it is the power of God unto salvation. It is abundantly possible to construct a would-be Gospel of which it would be as easy not to be ashamed as it is easy not to be ashamed of the Platonic philosophy, or of the Kantian. Into such "another Gospel" may be inserted sublime conceptions of God, and of man, and breathings after an immaculate purity, and sentiments of universal sympathy, and promises of a golden future, interminable and serene. But the true Gospel, by its own account, is a thing which man tends to be ashamed of, and which yet alone can come to him, and take him, and lift him up to God's own high places. And it is this because it insists upon approaching man as first a sinner, guilty, under sentence—no mere unfortunate, waylaid upon the by-paths of the Universe, fallen among thieves—but a criminal, and in the grasp of law.

Its purpose with him is not benignant only, but

glorious. It means to do much more than to restore him to himself. It will transfigure him; it will give him power to become a son of God; it will make him partaker of the divine Nature; it will seat him in the heavenly places with his Lord. He shall tread upon all the power of the enemy, more than conqueror through Him that loved him. He shall never die; he shall appear with Christ in glory; he shall be like Him, seeing Him as He is. But antecedent to all this, and in direct order to it, the Gospel has to deal with man as not an unfortunate, but a sinner. It has to stop his mouth of the last faltering self-justification, and to teach him how to put out a mere mendicant hand to take a mere free pardon, totally undeserved, and so to be welcomed in Another's Name, and henceforth to know no master, and no power, and no hope, beside Him who has loved him the unlovely, and given Himself for him the guilty.

And this is what "the flesh" is ashamed of. And this is the power of God unto salvation. And this is the inmost note and difference of the Gospel for the whole world, unalterable as the race of man and as the Christ of God. So it was in 1799; so it is today; so it shall be in the unknown twentieth century, yea, and *usque ad tubam*—till the trumpet shall sound, till the Lord shall come again, and all the saints with Him. Even so, come, Lord Jesus!

If His own words of commission are indeed our warrant, so it is. I have recited as our text that most dogmatic of His recorded instructions to His Church after His resurrection, in view of the evangelization of the world. The whole burden of the words is this—His dying work, His resurrection power, the sin of man shown in His light, the forgiveness of man given for His sake: "Thus it is written, that the Christ should suffer, and should rise again, and that repentance"—the recognition, the confession, the forsaking of sin—"and remission"—amnesty, pardon, welcome, peace with God —"should be preached in His name." All other blessings, but these first, and in that order. For these He suffered; for these He was exalted. He is enthroned, "a Prince and Saviour, to give repentance and remission."* And this, not to one race or type of manhood rather than to another. Semite, Hamite, Turanian, Aryan—all have sinned, and all must thus be called and blessed. The message was alike to "begin at Jerusalem," specimen and type of whole regions of the Orient, and to extend "to all nations" of every continent and every sea.

As the Master, so the servants. In the apostolic

* Acts v. 31.

writers we have chosen types of character profoundly varied. In the regions and races they address in speech, and in epistle, we have chosen samples of the world. The Hebrew is there, and the Athenian, the Roman, the Levantine, the Galatian Celt, the Phrygian of the remote Lycus, enamored of the theosophy of the remoter East. To them messages are sent by men as different in cast of character and trend of thought as Paul, and Peter, and John. But every messenger to every tribe and mission sends a Gospel which, however rich and varied, and locally adjusted in its circumference, is the same thing at its center; it is the preaching of the Cross. "First of all, Christ died for our sins; so we preach, whether it were I or they." "He nailed to His Cross the handwriting that was against us." "Ye were redeemed with the precious blood of Christ, the unspotted Lamb." "Christ was once offered to bear the sins of many." "We have an Advocate with the Father, and He is the propitiation for our sins, and for the sins of the whole world." "Thou wast slain, and hast redeemed us by Thy blood."*

"From error and misunderstanding," so runs the Litany of the Moravians, "from the loss of our glory

* 1 Cor. xv. 3; Col. ii. 14; 1 Pet. i. 19; Heb. ix. 28; 1 John ii. 2; Rev. v. 9.

in Thee, from coldness to Thy merits and Thy death, preserve us, gracious Lord and God."

Is this old Gospel of the Cross a narrow gospel? Yes; just as narrow as the gate and as the way of which our Master spoke of old. Is it a narrow Gospel? No; in its beating heart, warm with the blood of the Atonement, there lie, always ready for infinite expansion, all the blessings for eternity and for time which were lodged for us by the Father in the Son, and liberated for us by the sacrifice of His death; for ever blessed be His Name!

In that Name our missionaries, "the messengers of the Churches, and the glory of Christ," go to all the nations. They go to teach them many things, yea, "all things whatsoever He has commanded." They go to gather and to combine, to minister the Lord's ordinances, to build up men in the Lord's Body, to equip His disciples for His service; to lead them out into His holy war. But first and most they go to preach, and to glorify, His CROSS.

For themselves that Cross, borne for their own salvation, is divine peace and power for their suffering as for their witness. "In that sign they conquer." It is their victory beneath the tropic sun, and upon the arctic ice, in the long patience of the

30 THE OLD GOSPEL FOR THE NEW AGE.

manifold plowing and sowing, and in the joys of the harvest-home of souls. And it is all in all to them when the Master calls His beloved servant aside, and bids him bow down and glorify God by dying—in the shipwreck on the Indian deep, amidst the death-damps of the Niger, by gun-shot beside the lake of the Equator, by the rebel murderer's sword in Sierra Leone.

⁂ The references at the close are to the deaths of missionaries: Mrs. Smyth, Archdeacon Dobinson, Mr. G. L. Pilkington, and the Rev. W. J. Humphrey.

II

THE SECRET OF THE PRESENCE

Preached in the University Church, Cambridge

"Thou shalt hide them in the secret of Thy Presence."—Ps. xxxi. 20.

AND who are "they," of whom the prophet speaketh this? Is it a favored few, a selected and exempted remnant, whom the care of the Eternal shall insulate from the open world, and remove into the silence of the forests or the hills to contemplate and to adore? Is "the secret," "the covert," some curtained or cloistered circle where the wicked cease from troubling, and where there is leisure to be good? Is it a home with God beyond the grave in the land far off, where the righteous enters into the peace and light of immortality, resting upon his bed?* Is the promise restricted to priests and seers here, or to the just made perfect yonder? No, it is not so. The last preceding words tell us otherwise. The "they" of this golden oracle are all those who fear Him, all those who trust in Him.

* Isa. lvii. 2.

The humblest spiritual loyalist to God, the weakest and the weariest and the busiest, who hides himself in Him, who commits the way to Him, who commends the spirit to Him; this hidden life, this secret of the Presence—it is for even him.

And it is for him (we read again in the preceding sentence) as fearing thus, and as trusting thus, "before the sons of men." It is for those who avow the Lord as their King, and venture upon His promises, "before the sons of men." In the thick of human intercourse, amidst the shock and conflicts of human change, under the hot glare of human observation, out of doors amidst the dissonance of the common day—it is there that this wonderful promise of the Holy Ghost by the Psalmist is to take effect. For so it runs, "O how great is Thy goodness, which Thou hast laid up for them that fear Thee; which Thou hast wrought for them that trust in Thee before the sons of men. Thou shalt hide them in the secret of Thy Presence."

Such is the scope of the promise, "for them that fear Thee, them that trust in Thee." Such is the place of the promise, "before the sons of men."

I attempted last Sunday* to speak of that great fact of the Gospel, the autocratic rights of our Lord

---

* The sermon referred to is not included in this volume.

Jesus Christ over us, and His call to us for an unconditional surrender of the whole of life to Him. I aimed all along to remind you that the true place for such a surrender and its issues is the field of common life, "the next thing," "the duty that lies near," the circumstances which as a fact are ours. Surrender to Jesus Christ is not a thing reserved for exciting occasions or artificial conditions. It is for the Christian man to-day, under the environment of this time present, in our own generation, be its obstacles and its problems what they may, so long as they are not of our choosing, but of the will of God. And now I point you again to that familiar field. I invite you out, as it were, among the sons of men. And I say, as we survey that scene of realities and of trial, that there, even there, is the intended place not only for a genuine recognition of the rights of Jesus Christ, but for a profound enjoyment of His presence. That bright secret is no curiosity for a spiritual museum. It lives and moves; it is made for use. It is revealed, it is offered, it is given, to be worn and wielded amidst the wear and tear of all that is present, of all that is practical around us as we are.

Such is one link between our theme of last week and this. Surrender and the Presence, the Lord's entire ownership over us and His invitation to us to live concealed in the Secret of His Presence—these both, according to God in His Word, are things altogether meant to work and reign in real life. Nor is this the only tie between these two spiritual facts. They not only walk the same path; they are locked there by strong embraces into one. They are, I may say, two poles of one spiritual sphere. Surrender is the negative thing where the Presence is the positive. Surrender is the man's turning from himself to his Redeemer, dropping in the act the base plunder of self-love, and stretching out arms capacious, because empty, towards Him. The Presence is the Redeemer's meeting the man with the fulness of Himself, with the gift of nothing less than Himself to the creature who brings nothing but necessities and submission. So the two spiritual facts by their own nature eternally complement each other. We have all often confessed this, aye, and ourselves claimed to act upon it, as we have knelt, believing and receiving, at the Table of the Feast of Christ. "Here we *offer and present* unto Thee ourselves, our souls and bodies, humbly beseeching Thee that *all we* may be *fulfilled, filled full*, with Thy grace."

That glorious complex, Surrender and the Presence, is the liberty of the life of grace and its inviolable peace and its ever-springing power. In that supreme paradox, the Gospel, these sacred paradoxes have their vital place. An absolute submission is the secret of a perfect freedom. A supernatural peace, an inward dwelling in the divine Covert, is the secret of a life wonderfully enabled for holy energy and action along the daily path.

But now, to look direct upon this latter, this hiding in the secret of His Presence before the sons of men.

The promise is akin, as you well know, to a whole host of promises. "Thou wilt keep him in perfect peace whose mind is stayed on Thee"; "My presence shall go with thee, and I will give thee rest"; "He leadeth me beside the waters of repose"; "The peace of God which passeth all understanding shall keep your hearts"; "Peace I leave with you, My peace I give unto you; in Me ye shall have peace"; "Come unto Me, all ye that labor, and I will rest you; ye shall find rest unto your souls."

Here first observe the paradox of such words, then their promise. The paradox is, as I have said, that the Christian life is, on the one hand, meant to know no rest or holiday from obedience to the law of duty, from hourly "serving our generation in the will of God"; yet, on the other hand, at the very heart of such a life there is always to be this mysterious stillness, this secret place of peace. Not from an inner tumult of wrestling energies is to come that life's true power, but from this hidden calm. The unfatigued willingness to suffer, to sacrifice, to labor, to sympathize, to bestow, is to leap continually from a spring in itself as silent as it is profound. A life all activity (or perhaps all suffering) at the circumference, and revolving amidst the tangled things of the common hour, is yet to move upon a central point of rest—

> "With inoffensive pace that spinning sleeps
> On the soft axle."

The world, the flesh, the tempter—all will be present, formidable parts of the Christian's circumstances; but "Thou shalt hide him in the secret of Thy Presence." Thronging duties may press him hard, but "Thou shalt hide him in the secret of Thy Presence." Sufferings of body, anguish of spirit, may strike upon the life. And grace is no anæsthetic; the Christian is no Stoic: he is follower and member of the Lord of Bethany and of Gethsemane; he feels, he grieves indeed; yet, "Thou shalt hide him in the secret of Thy Presence." Or look another way altogether. Take life in its most vivid, its most pleasing interests and occupations. So these things lie for the man in the line of the will of God, and so the man fears Him and trusts Him before the sons of men; the paradox of grace is that in these things also "Thou shalt hide them in the secret of Thy Presence."

It is indeed an enigma, as is almost every other great fact of the religion of the Bible. But none the less, it is, it is indeed, *a promise*. "Thou shalt hide them"; "I will give thee rest"; "Ye shall find rest unto your souls"; "The peace of God which passeth all understanding shall keep your hearts."*

Those last sacred words, remember, are *a promise*. We are accustomed to hear them in another and indeed a soul-moving form. As the hour of worship closes, as the communicants prepare to leave the precincts of the Table, when

"The feast, though not the love, is past and gone,"

then the pastor lets the flock go with the invocation upon them of the peace of God. It is an invocation rich in significance and power. But do not forget that its divine original in the Philippian Epistle is not an invocation, but a precise and positive promise. True, it is a promise under conditions—above all, under the condition that in everything we make known our requests to God. But that granted, then there follows nothing less than this certainty and guarantee: "The peace of God *shall* keep your hearts." Need I count it out of place and time here

* Phil. iv. 7.

to point to that strong future tense, that wonderful "shall," and ask myself, and ask my brethren, if we have proved it true? I will ask the question, I will humbly press it on the soul. Here is the voice of God, the warrant of God: Have we made our claim under it, and found it to mean what it says? Ah, I am speaking to many, well I know, who have so done and have so found. For myself, so far as a sinful man may venture personally to affirm, I know enough to dare to say the ground is good, if a man use it lawfully. There *is* a peace of God, able indeed to keep, to safeguard the weakest and the most treacherous heart. There is a Presence that makes at life's center a stillness pregnant with positive and active blessing. There is a "fulfilling" that can counterwork the fulness of the thronging hours and enable men, in the stress of real life, to live behind it all with Jesus Christ, while they are all the while alert and attentive for the next call of duty, and the next. The Christian is indeed to be ever seeking, ever aspiring upward, "not as though he had already attained." He is to avoid as his most deadly poison that subtle spiritual Pharisaism which plumes itself upon a supposed advanced experience, and presumes to compare itself with others, and hesitates, if but for a moment, to prostrate itself in confession and penitence before the awful, the blessed holiness of God. But none the less, the Christian is called to a great rest as well as to a great aspiration. He is called to a great thanksgiving as well as to a deep confession. He is called, he is commanded to an entrance into the peace of God. It is not to be the *habit* of his soul to say, or to sing, that he *should* be happy if he *could* cast his care on his Redeemer, and sink in His almighty arms. It is to be his, on the ground of all the promises, to do it and *to be* at rest in God.

Conditions there are, indeed, to that great peace; so we have remembered. But they are conditions each of them, in its nature, a heavenly blessing. There is the condition of godly fear. There is the condition of humble trust. There is the condition of trust thus *before the sons of men*—let not that be forgotten. There is the condition of coming direct to Jesus Christ, to take the yoke of His word and will. There is the condition of looking unto Him. There is the condition of watching and of prayer. But are these things a complicated and a grievous burthen, a bundle of arbitrary exactions? They are so many forms only of that one great condition to our finding what is laid up for us in our Lord, the condition of coming into directest contact with Himself, and there abiding. Such contact, in God's own order, liberates into the believing suppliant the virtues of Jesus Christ. Not peace only, but "His peace," is given.

It is a wonderful thing to be permitted to watch a life which you have reason to know is hid in the secret of the Presence of the Lord. Some few years ago I met a good man, humble and gentle, a missionary to Eastern Africa. He abode in the Presence. I could not but see it. I heard him tell, with the eloquence of entire simplicity, how, in the tropical wilderness, in the deep night, he had waited for and shot the ranging lion which had long been the unresisted terror of a village clan. It could not be the will of God, he reasoned, that this beast should lord it over men; and so, as it were in the way of Christian business, he went forth and put it to death. And then I watched that man, a guest in my own house, under the very different test of the inconvenience of missing a train; and the secret of the Presence was as surely with him then as when he had lain quietly down to sleep in his tent on the lonely field, to be roused only by the sound of the lion's paw as it rent the earth at the open door.

I have marked the secret of the Presence as it ruled and triumphed in young lives around me here. I recall a conversation on the subject. It was with a friend and student of my own, a loving Christian, but also an ardent and vigorous athlete. Could the peace of God keep him, he wondered and inquired, when the strong temper was ready to take fire in the rush and struggle of the game? And the answer came in a quiet, thankful word, three days later: "Yes, I asked Him; I trusted Him; and He kept me altogether."

I have watched lives in which the secret of the Presence has been drawn around mental studies and competitions. It has made the man care for his subject not less but more. It has made him not less but more intent to do well, to do better, to do best; αἰὲν ἀριστεύειν καὶ ὑπείροχον ἔμμεναι ἄλλων. But it has taken the poison out of competition by bringing into it Jesus Christ. And so has come the honest aim to win knowledge and to train faculty for Him, and to lay up just such prestige as might perchance subserve His ends in His disciple's life. And equally and at the same time it has prepared the man's spirit for the blessed bitterness of disappointment.

The secret of the Presence can assert itself in our times, as of old, in the awful hours of life. It can give now, as long ago, to the suffering confessor those *divinas martyrum consolationes* which a prisoner of the Reformation found, with astonished joy, filling not another's soul, but his own, in the grim dungeon. A few years ago, in a mountain town in the province of Fuh-kien, in China, two men, recent converts to the Lord, were beset by a furious mob and hung up each to a tree, to be beaten there to death. The elder, a sturdy peasant, who had often pleaded with his neighbors, even to tears, for Christ, fearing for the firmness of his younger friend, called out to him: "Do not forget Him who died for us; do not deny Him." "But, indeed," said the other, as he very simply told the story soon after to his friend and mine, the Rev. Robert Stewart,* "indeed he needed not to say it; the Holy Ghost so filled me that I felt no fear or trouble." Rescue by a detachment of Chinese soldiery came just in time—not too soon to have allowed the confessors fully to prove, not the bitterness of death, but the glorious secret of the Presence.

Now, God be thanked for conspicuous spiritual miracles such as this and such as that great martyr-triumph not many years ago† in inner Africa, by the shore of the Victoria Lake, when those young saints of God ascended the fiery chariot, singing with loud voices the praises of their Saviour upon their own red funeral pile. His arm is not shortened that it cannot save, even in such straits as these; the

* Afterwards himself martyred, July, 1895.   † 1885.

secret of His Presence is as powerful now as when it worked open miracle in the Chaldean furnace. But it is often well to turn from the swelling thoughts suggested by the exceptional and the heroic in the records of the Gospel, to the sober questions of the uneventful lifetime; to the common scene and the transfiguring power of the blessed secret there. And as I do so, a name, a face, a presence, rises on my soul. I see one whose life for long, long years I watched indeed with microscopic nearness. I see a Christian woman, surrendered at all hours to the never-ceasing doing of the nearest and least romantic duty; open on every side to every appeal for aid, for toil, for love; the summer sunshine of the full and busy home; the friend of every needing, every sinning life, in the wide, poor parish; experienced indeed in the pure joys which come to hearts that forget themselves, but called again and again to agonies of sorrow. And I see this life, in its radiant but unconscious beauty, at once and equally and with a living harmony, practical down to the smallest details, and filled with God; open to every whisper, to every touch, that said "I want you," and hidden, deep hidden, morning, noon and night, in the secret of the Presence. That life was a long miracle, "and long the track of light it left behind it," to the praise of the glory of His grace who shone out from its blessed depths. Let me give Him thanks for it, indeed. It is not past; it is not lost; only hidden a little deeper than before with Christ in God, where

> "Yet once more I trust to have
> Full sight of her in heaven, without restraint."

In Christ, a son needs not to say, *Mater, ave atque vale.* The secret of the Presence includes both worlds and folds them into one.

My brethren, as we draw our meditation toward its close, I revert to the precise wording of my text: "Thou shalt hide them in the secret of Thy Presence [*b'sether paneyka*], in the covert of Thy Countenance." It is a glorious stroke of divine poetry —the covert, the secret, of His countenance. We find kindred phrases elsewhere in the precious Psalter—the shelter of the brooding Wings of the Eternal, the abode in His mighty Shadow. But this phrase stands out as a peculiar treasure—"the secret of Thy Countenance." There is no shadow here; it is "a privacy of glorious light." And what a light! It is light that lives. It is a photosphere, within which opens upon the happy inmate the sweetness and the response of a personal, while eternal, smile. It is not it, but He. It is not a sanctuary, but a Saviour, and a Father seen full in Him, giving to the soul nothing less than Himself indeed in vivid intercourse. It is the Lord, according to that dear promise of the Paschal evening, coming to manifest Himself, and to make His abode with the man, and to dwell in him, and he in Him.* It means the spirit's sight of Him that is invisible. It means a life, lived not in Christianity but in Christ, who is our life.

And thus the word takes us—out in the open, out before the sons of men and amidst the strife of tongues—to the deep central glory of the Gospel, that it may be ours in humble, wondering possession. The Gospel, the εὐαγγέλιον—what is it? Subordinately, it is many things. It is the revelation of the redemption of our nature by the work of the Incarnate Son wrought once and forever for us. It is the message of the unutterable mercy of that pardon which moved the prophet's awestricken wonder: "Who is a God like unto Thee, that pardoneth iniquity?"† It is the message of the bringing of the guilty in penitent faith into the sublime amnesty of the Holy One, because of His own gift of His own Begotten, who died, the Just for the unjust, the Propitiation for our sins. It is the message of the more than restoration of our fallen na-

* John xiv. 23. † Micah vii. 18.

ture in our second Head. It is the bringing of life and immortality out from shadows into the light.*
It is the revelation of wonderful possibilities of benefit and blessing for this life present in even its temporary aspects, ever since it has been possible to say of all men, yea, of the lowest and the worst of human persons or human tribes, *"for whom Christ died."* But the inmost glory of the Gospel, the mysterious central brightness of its message—what is it? It is the giving by God of Himself to man. It is man's union, and then communion, with none other than God in Christ. For this was given prophecy and preparation, patriarchs and priests and kings. For this was Bethlehem and Nazareth and Golgotha and Joseph's Garden and the Hill of the Ascension and the fiery shower of Pentecost. For this was righteousness imputed and holiness imparted and the immortal redemption of our body revealed. Here, and no lower, from our point of sight, lies the final cause of all the saving process. It was in order that God, with infinite rightness, and with all the willingness of eternal love, might give Himself to man and dwell in man and walk in him and shine out from him, in measure here, hereafter perfectly.

So we will come and take, for He stands in act

* 2 Tim. i. 10.

THE SECRET OF THE PRESENCE. 47

to give. So it shall be ours to say, in the sweet English of a Hindoo Christian poetess:

"In the secret of His Presence how my soul delights to hide!
Ah! how hallowed are the lessons that I learn at Jesus' side!"

We are invited, here and now, in Jesus Christ, into the secret of the Countenance of God. To enter there in the blessed Name is not presumption; it is submission. And the result, the practice—what will it be? The humblest walk of duty; the simplest and least ostentatious, but most genuine denial of the life of self; the daily up-taking of the unpretentious cross; something always to do or to be for others and for the Lord; while in it and over it and behind it all, rules a peace which does in sober fact pass understanding, keeping heart and thought, the safeguard of the secret of the Countenance of our King.

III.

THE BRIGHT AND MORNING STAR

Preached in the University Church, Cambridge, at the opening of the Academic Year.
"I am the bright and morning Star."—Rev. xxii. 16.

This is the last place in Scripture where the glorious Saviour bears witness to Himself. A few lines below He once more promises to return: "Behold, I come quickly." But of His own words regarding His own excellence and majesty this is the last: "I am the bright and morning Star."

The hours of the great vision were almost over. The Apostle who had walked with Jesus long ago as His daily friend had been entranced for awhile into an experience of His presence as He now reigned in "the power of an endless life"; and at length the trance was closing. An influence altogether from God had been imprinting on John's soul the messages to the Churches and the future of the Church; and now at the end the spiritual Voice has still this work to say; the Lord speaks of Himself once more. Perhaps the shadows of literal night were rolling from the rock of Patmos, and the literal day-star shone out in the region of the dawn. But, however, the spiritual view and the inner word were all of the light and of the day—"I am the bright and morning Star."

Our blessed Lord speaks here in a manner which is all His own. Nothing is more deeply characteristic of His utterances from first to last than His witness to Himself. It is one of the main phenomena of the Gospel, most perplexing on the theory of unbelief, most truth-like on the theory of belief, this *self-witness* of the Man of humility and sorrows. Sacred Exemplar of all that we commonly call self-denial, Jesus yet presents Himself always and unalterably in terms of self-assertion, and such self-assertion as must mean either Deity, however in disguise, or a delusion (may He forgive the word if its mere mention is irreverent), moral as well as mental, of infinite depth. "I am the Truth; I am the Life; I am the Bread of Life; I AM";* such is His tone.

And here we have the same tone, perfectly maintained, as the same voice speaks again from amidst the realities of the Unseen. The imagery, indeed, is lifted from earth to heaven. He who is the genial Vine and the laborious Shepherd now also reveals

* John viii. 58.

Himself as the Star of stars in a spiritual sky. But the novelty of the glorious term only conveys the truth which had always stood in the very front of the testimony of Jesus—the truth of His own sacredness and glory; the doctrine that He, the Son of the Father, is the ultimate peace and hope and joy of the soul of man.

Let us inquire a little into this divine utterance. Many treasures must lie hid in such a testimony so spoken. Some of them, however few, we may hope to make sure of as we go.

"I am the STAR." For the moment we take the sentence in this abbreviated form, for it will suggest to us something of the reason for the use of the starry metaphor at all. "I am the Star." Why the Star? Most certainly the word, with all its radiant beauty, is no mere flight of fancy. Prophecy, not poetry, gives us these last oracles of the Bible. If we need a ready proof, we have only to recall the clause just preceding, "I am the root and offspring of David," words which are heavy with the golden weight of prophecy and prophetic history; part of the long testimony borne by Messiah Himself to the divine nature and structure of those Scriptures which had, as a matter of recorded and verifiable fact, begotten the astonishing phenomenon of the definite expectation of His first Advent. In close contact

THE BRIGHT AND MORNING STAR.

with that sentence occur the words before us: "I am the Star." Here also, then, is an appeal to the prophets. And among the prophecies in which stars form the symbol there is but one which can be thought to point to Messiah—the prophecy of Balaam. Balaam, as he heard "the words of God, and saw the vision of the Almighty,"* had heard of a mysterious Person, or at least a mysterious Power, strong to conquer and to save, and had seen the prospect figured to his soul as a Star, destined in other days to rise from the horizon of Israel. And the belief of the Jewish Church, before and in the lifetime of Jesus, was that the Star of this old prediction was the King Messiah.

No doubt the import of Balaam's words has been variously explained. No doubt the whole doctrine of definitely predictive inspiration has been, and is, laboriously denied. But do we believe that these words of the Apocalypse are themselves a divine reality? Do we believe that both in, and thus after, "the days of His flesh" Jesus undertook not only to teach, but to foretell? And do we believe that He was, and is, all that He claimed to be? Then we have passed the point at which for any *a priori* reasons we can think it seriously difficult

* Num. xxiv. 4, 17.

to believe that He had been already foretold, however long before, as the Star of Jacob.

"I am the Star." Prophecy, then, spoke of Messiah thus. The word indicated His kingly dignity, touched and glorified with the light of Deity, or of Divinity at least. So the Lord takes it up here. He claims here to be the mystic *King,* immortal, spiritual, divine; the regal Conqueror, quelling His enemies and possessing His redeemed. This is what appears under other forms in other and earlier passages of the Apocalypse. "He had a name written, King of kings"; the Lamb is "in the midst of the throne," which is "the throne of God and of the Lamb."

But now we look further into the text. It not only claims the ancient prophecy for Jesus as the King of the new Israel; it expands that prophecy, and brings truth out of truth from within it. For the Saviour does not only assert Himself to be the Star, the bright Star; his presentation of the glorious metaphor has in it something new and special; "I am the Morning Star."

Why was not the word "star" left alone in the utterance? In pointing to Messiah as the star, were not the ideas of brilliancy and elevation and all that is ethereal sufficient? No, not sufficient. Messiah Himself so qualifies the word by this one wonderful epithet as to show Himself as not the King simply, but the King of Morning, around whom gather and shall gather forever all things that belong to tenderest hope and youngest vigor and most cheerful aspiration; such beginnings as shall eternally develop, shall never contract into fixity nor decline. He claims, where He indeed is King, to be the secret of such *juvenescence* as nothing else can ever give to the finite spirit. For His Israel He claims to be the ever-blessed Antithesis to all that has to do with decay and ruin, to all the woes and weakness of melancholy, to all "profitless regrets and longings vain." Not that He bids His follower crush pain and ignore bereavement and forget the past. But He asserts Himself the Master, the King of a future which will far more than make amends for the discipline of the present. And meanwhile, being the Eternal One, He is always so present with His own as to put them already into vital connection with that future, and to pour its strength and joy into their life this hour.

"I am the MORNING STAR." Such in part is the import of this last testimony of Jesus to Himself. It reminds His happy disciple that the beloved Lord is no mere name of tender recollection, no dear relic of a perished time, to be drawn sometimes in silence from its casket and clasped with the aching fondness and sprinkled with the hot tears of hopeless memory. He is not Hesperus who sets, but Phosphorus who rises, springing into the sky through the earliest dawn; the pledge of reviving life and growing light and all the energies and all the pleasures of the happy day. And the word speaks of a kind of joy for which the open noon would not be so true a simile. It suggests the joys of hope along with those of fruition; a happiness in which one of the deep elements is always the thought of something yet to be revealed; light with more light to follow, joy to expand into further joy, as the dawn passes into the morning and then into the day.

We have matter here, then, for some thankful thoughts on the blessings of light and happiness and vigor and hope which are bound up with the true idea of the religion of the Lord Jesus Christ. Here we are reminded how remote from melancholy are its principles and its motives. Here, indeed, is One able to guide and enliven and develop the whole of existence for His disciple; not only to prop his dying head, but to animate the fullest energies of his strongest prime; and then again, able with persistent grace to be His blessing to the last, shedding a morning light over the decline and shadows of advancing years.

Let us take up some of these aspects of the truth of our text and think awhile over their details.

i. First, then, we are reminded here that, as "His commandments are not grievous," so the motives He gives to animate His loving follower to obedience are not melancholy. I would not be mistaken. The religion of Jesus Christ is very far from teaching that "there is nothing in God to dread." What language can outdo the terror of the warnings of the Saviour when He speaks of what is, according to Him, the sequel, the necessary sequel, of that wide road on which so many travel? But this is not to say that His motive principles are things of gloom. It is not melancholy that looks direct at realities and acts upon the view. It is not melancholy to bid us gaze in earnest on the unfathomable mystery, which is also the iron fact, of sin, and tell us without reserve what sin must lead to in the spiritual nature of things. Not to do this would indeed be melancholy, for it would be the reticence of a dreadful iron. But the Lord, who speaks about the abyss, does so that He may speak, with infinite earnestness and the smile of His own welcome, about the rescue and the remedy. And that remedy is no shadowed secret, no nocturnal initiation; it is the morning light of the knowledge of Himself. The life eternal, the destruction of the second death, is the knowledge of Himself; and to know Him is to live in light indeed. It is to touch a sympathy boundless alike in its tenderness and in its power. It is to deal always and everywhere with One who is not poetic legend, but the central Rock of history. He has proved Himself in the fields of fact to be a reality forever; and He is exercising at this hour in Human experience a personal influence too vast, too manifold, too peculiar, to be explained by any mere memory of recorded and departed power.

He being such, and such being the knowledge of Him, what are in brief His sacred principles for the man who seeks Him? In their essence, simply these: first to trust Him, then to follow Him. The soul is directed for its repose and its life far from subjective bewilderments of thought to things objective altogether, because altogether His, not ours; to the blood of His Cross, to the power of His resurrection. And for its progress, for its hope, it is directed still outward from itself, because still to Him; into the ethereal open air of His will, His possession, His glory. It is called every day and every hour to a surrender of itself to Him; to the daylight reality of a true self-dedication to One who does indeed reserve to Himself the right to be silent when He pleases, but who has proved Himself worthy of an absolute trust in regard of His perfection of wisdom and power and love.

ii. Again, this glorious epithet of the Star of Salvation, this morning-word, reminds us that not for a part only, but for the whole of the earthly course, early as well as late, late as well as early, Jesus Christ is the true light to lighten every man. Not for the sick-room only and for the death-bed is His Gospel good. Let us often thank God that it *is* good there. Many of us have stood and watched in the face of others all that can be seen of death, perhaps while the very "desire of our eyes" was being taken from us*; there we have felt a little of the mighty difference between the moment before death and the moment after. Or perhaps our own life, even in its early prime, has hung in the balance, and some of "the powers of the world to come" have touched us through the thin curtain of extremest weakness. One religion only will do at such a time: the religion which has really dealt with sin and with death; the Gospel of a Redeemer who has willed to die beneath the rod of His own law, and has risen again with the keys of the Unseen forever in His hand.

* Ezek. xxiv. 16.

> "Jesus, I cast myself on Thee,
>   Mighty and merciful to save;
> Thou wilt go down to death with me,
>   And gently lay me in the grave."

There is but one religion which can make such language as this the natural speech of its followers. Let us be glad that there is one.

But this same religion is not only the last light for dying eyes: it is the star of *the morning* of even this lower life. There is that in it—or rather in HIM who is His own Religion—which is, of all things, fitted to enter with harmonious power into all the confiding joys of childhood, and into all the wide excursions and strong ascents of youthful thought and will. One condition does the Lord propose to the young soul, as to all souls—the condition of submission to Himself. And where, through His grace, that condition, in its true sense, is accepted, there an element essentially of strength and gladness will be found to develop within the life; a cheerful assurance of a companionship most warm and tender, because divine, of a vivid sympathy meeting every true need of grief or happiness, of a wisdom which concerns itself with every detail of every day, of an affection to which the best endearments of earth can but point as to their glorious archetype. And above all this, and with it all, there will be the power of the known presence of an invisible but awful purity, and of the spoken promise—in connection with that presence—of a final life of deathless joy. And, without a law of unbending holiness above it, without an immortal hope before it, the gladness of the most youthful heart carries, lurking beneath it, the sure causes of gloom and failure and melancholy and decay.

Will my brethren who have just entered on their academic course suffer me, in the sincerity of respectful earnestness, to point this appeal direct to them? Would you have this new life of yours rich beyond all reckoning in possible happiness and good? Would you have it not merely safe, but glad, glad with a pleasure which will bear looking into, and fruitful, as it is meant to be, of results full of pleasure for yourselves and others? The sky for most of you is bright with the morning of this world. Not that many have not already tasted something of the sadness of things. Many a man comes up here for his first University term experienced already in loss and sorrow. But these burthens in their fulness cannot yet have come to the most among you, thank God! and the hope and joy of life prevail. Well, do you really care to perpetuate hope and to make joy immortal? Do you care for that which will be in you a well of youth springing up into the endless youth of the sons of the Resurrection? Then assure yourselves of Jesus Christ, who is the Morning Star. Acquaint yourselves with Him in that special and definite contact of faith which, finding Him to be Saviour, inevitably also apprehends Him as Friend and as Master. In Him so known you will find that which will lend an immortal brightness to all other things which, being pure, are capable of reflecting immortality. You will find in Him an influence which will intensify all just enjoyment and will glorify all healthful knowledge by connecting it with things to come—an influence *without* which nothing else—no, nothing—can be safe from impurity and decay; no social pleasure, no delights of reason or imagination, no charm of letters or of art. Take up these things and leave your Lord behind, and you will be only carrying your possessions to their burial, with your face to the region of disappointment, weariness and final loss. You will be on your way to find the "hollowness"—on these terms—"of all delight"; to be at length, above all things, tired of your own principles of life and your own tone of thought. But take up these things, as you can, and make sure of your Lord with them, as you may; receive them and use them for Him, and you are bearing your possessions along the path of life and light and day, straight towards the rich, eternal issues of all the training, whether of affliction or gladness, through which you pass under the leading of Him who is the Morning Star of the Epiphany of glory.

iii. In a few short years there may, there must, come over you the sense of an approaching maturity and fixity as to earthly conditions of life and action. You will find, soon or late, that, as to this world, your rate of movement in work and in enjoyment is no longer what it was. But if, indeed, "Christ dwells in your hearts by faith," there will be a charm there which will not only console you under the change, but will glorify it to you. As eternity approaches you will more distinctly see the connexion between it and time. The appointed task, even under the burthen of the failure of outward power, will be met by you as those only can meet it who know that all things are links in the indissoluble plan of an eternal Friend, and that the veil is already parting which shuts out for a season the open view of the perfection and acceptability of all His will.

Grace can work strange and beautiful contradictions to the natural decay of our sense of enjoyment of external things. I know of one whose life had been spent in a city rich with splendid monuments of the past, and it had been a life of dull indifference to all things noble and fair. But his Redeemer at length became a reality to the man, who then said that never before had he *seen* the beauty and grandeur of the place where he had lived so long. They had never truly come to his perception—till he discovered the light of "the love of God which is in Christ Jesus our Lord."

So we have traced a little way some of the suggestions of this heavenly utterance. We have remembered the divine, the dear Redeemer, whose Gospel is the very antithesis and antidote to that melancholy which is always akin to perplexity and weakness. We have seen in Him the true Secret for a perfect security and perpetuity in the days of life's full vigor, and then as the Revealer of that glorious continuity of time with eternity which keeps the cancer of despondency out of our earthly maturity and decline.

May we not, in conclusion, move a step further, and find here a promise which is concerned also immediately with the heavenly world itself? He who here calls himself the Star is elsewhere called the Sun.* We might think that he speaks here as, in a certain sense, His own forerunner—the Firstborn from the dead, whose own resurrection is the heralding of His own final triumph. But it seems truer to the analogy of His other metaphoric titles to view

* Mal. iv. 2.

this designation as belonging properly not to any passing phase of His majesty, but to its essence for ever. What elsewhere He claims to be, that in perpetuity He is. On the Throne, as truly as on the Cross, He is still the Lamb.* In the fields of heaven He is still the Shepherd, "leading His flock to the living fountains of water."† And surely in the upper skies He will likewise be *for ever* the Star of Morning; the eternal Pledge of a life which will be forever young, of energies which will accumulate without end, of a service before the throne which will always deepen in its ardor and its triumph, of discoveries in the knowledge of the Eternal and His love which will carry the experience of the Blessed from glory on to glory in a succession which can never close.

Avidi et semper pleni, quod habent desiderant.

"At Thy right hand there are pleasures for evermore."

"Ever filled and ever seeking, what they have they still desire;
Hunger there shall fret them never, nor satiety shall tire;
Still enjoying whilst aspiring, in their joy they still aspire."‡

---

* Rev. vii. 17. † Rev. vii. 17.
‡ From the Latin of Damiani (eleventh century), translated in "Chronicles of the Schönberg-Cotta Family."

IV

SELF-SURRENDER AND ITS POSSES-SIONS—I

Preached in the University Church, Cambridge, at the opening of the Academic Year.

"Ye are not your own."—1 Cor. vi. 19.
"All things are yours."—1 Cor. iii. 21.

To-day, and again a week hence, I am called to this pulpit to address my brethren in our Master's name. Some continuity between the two occasions seems desirable, and we shall find it in the contrasted messages of my double text, in its "not your own" and its "all things yours." I read the two together to-day, and shall do so again next Sunday; we shall be reminded thus that under the contrast, under the contradiction, lies a strong connection. The "not your own" and the "all things yours" are not only statements, both true, but truths which act and react on one another, "unto life eternal." But we will also, in some sort, take the two apart for study. To-day our main attention shall be given to "Ye are not your own."

"Ye are not your own." And who are *"ye"*? All bearers of the Christian name. First, of course, in the immediate intention of the passage, the members of the mission Church at Corinth, about the year 57 of our Lord; but then also, of course, all who succeed them in their Christian position, therefore ourselves to-day. It is not an inner and selected circle only; that is not the thought here. There is place indeed, momentous place, for that view of things; but that place is not here. To the baptized man as such, taken on his profession, to the rank and file of the community, taken on their profession, as much as to the most advanced and exalted of their leaders and exemplars, this word was spoken then, "Ye are not your own." And it is spoken so to-day.

I emphasize this manifest fact in order to be as practical as possible in approaching, for myself and my brethren, the conscience and the will. Too often we are tempted, perhaps without any explicit avowal to ourselves that we are doing so, to relegate the really searching demands of the Gospel to the full obedience, not of all Christians, but of some. The most diverse religious tenets may give occasion for such thoughts, or may seem to lend them an excuse. They may be colored by convictions upon the divine election; or they may be connected with a theory that in Christianity there is an allowed lower level for the multitude, and a reservation of "counsels of perfection" for the few. But theory has often little or nothing to do with the matter—it is the subtle error of the will. The man hesitates or declines to own that the claims of Jesus Christ are impartial upon all who bear the Christian name, because, whatever his opinions, he does not like the claims.

"What, then! Is this meant seriously and indeed? Am I only a piece of personal property after all? I am quite ready to own an environment of obligation around me. I have no wish to revolt, certainly not theoretically to revolt, against a large range of duties which I acknowledge as much as you do—duties of truthfulness, duties of human kindness, duties of reverence and worship toward the Unseen. I recognize the fact and mystery of '*I ought*' in many matters outside these. I do not claim to float *in vacuo*, and to live merely at my pleasure, as regards the use of my time and of my money, and the discipline of my mind, with a view to an employment of it for which somehow I am responsible. To be, so to speak, a constitutional subject under a moderate government of duty, reasonably to consider other people in the concrete, and to own myself in a general way responsible in the abstract—this is as it should be. But you tell me much more than this. You affirm that *I*, not only my surroundings and certain relations and obligations which they generate, *but I,* am 'not my own.' I am willing, standing at the center, to treat with respect the circumference and its contents. But your words invade the center; they seize on *me,* they dare to describe me as a purchase, as a possession, as the implement of another's centripetal will. They label me a bondman, a slave—abhorrent word!—no free contracting party who may, and who will, be loyal within his rights, but one who has no rights at all, in respect of his being not his own. If you mean what you say, you mean for me immensely much. You throw the lien of this tremendous ownership over my whole being, over my whole time, over my whole possessions. The logic of such claims goes inexorably far. If *I* am purchased, all that is contingent upon me goes with the bargain. The slave of old could own nothing, for he was owned; his clothes and tools, as well as his body, belonged absolutely to his buyer. So, according to you, all that goes with me, all that is thrown in along with me, is not my own; for *I* am torn from my center, and given over *in toto* to another's hands. It is a hard saying; who can hear it?"

My brethren, I have attempted to report, as it were, the protests, perhaps the avowed and energetic protests, of many a human heart. I am supposing, not what we should popularly call a bad case. This is not a man definitely resolved on wrong, or stupidly insensible to the cry of conscience—a life which has "altogether broken the yoke and burst the bonds." Here rather is one who would claim, and justly, much of our respect and our regard. It is a character largely attentive to common duties, perhaps strongly attached to the high idea of duty in a certain valuable degree; a life from which we might conceivably draw useful and even inspiring suggestions, as we watch the probity and the kindliness, and listen to the honest utterances of good-sense and generous feeling. But even in face of such a life, I do claim, not the less but the more because of its conditions and of its protests, that our Lord Jesus Christ and His Apostles altogether refuse to rest *content* with the position. They do affirm—HE does affirm—that this man, all the while, is, in fact, not his own; he is "bought, with a price." They do say that "Christ died, and rose, and revived," not only to shower upon this man benignant gifts, as indeed He did, but also to be his autocratic Lord, whether he is dead or living. They do uncompromisingly inform him that his true position, in respect of his Redeemer, includes in it—deep within it, at its center, at its heart—the relation of the implement to the artificer, of the bondman to the owner, of the limb to the will. They will not let him rest in a dream of constitutional and contracting loyalty.

They tell him that he is not his own, and they make it plain to him in a hundred ways that if the fact stands thus (and the Cross and the Resurrection are their immediate evidence that it does), then the only ultimate and adequate rest and rightness for the man is to assent and consent cordially to the fact. Is the branch for the tree? Its life and freedom lie in its absolute cohesion. Is the limb for the body? Dislocate it, and it is in misery; amputate it, and it is in corruption. Set it, and let it be employed in its articulated subjection; it lives, it glows, it plays, as it works, in a perfect life.

"*I belong.*" This is one of the great primal watchwords of the Christian life. May they not all be reduced in the last resort to two—"*I believe, I belong*"? "I believe," receiving my Redeemer in His love and glory; "I belong," giving myself to Him. Omit the one, omit the other, and you have a half Christianity—"another Gospel, which is not another." Confess them both, in the presence of God, and before the face of man in the realities of life, and Christ shall form Himself and shall glorify Himself in you.

We have already begun to remind ourselves, with that sort of reminder which only puts into order the well-known contents of the mind, that the stern watchword is, after all, pregnant of liberty and rest;

for we have already been passing from the thought of who he is who is not his own, into the recollection of who He is whose own He is. We might have lingered longer upon the other aspects. It might have been well, did time serve us, to spread out much larger, and think over much more in detail the awful, the sacred, the infinitely salutary truth of *the duty* of surrender. We might have discussed awhile the abstract fitness of the creature's consent to its totally dependent and obliged relation to the Creator, the strict impossibility of its being right within itself till it is right in its internal attitude towards Him. But if we would see the glory of God so as to live and to love, we must make haste to see it "in the face of Jesus Christ." In Him—blessed be His name!—eternal Right draws near, and, never for a moment losing its pure majesty, transfigures itself with a wonderful smile into eternal Love. In Jesus Christ duty (no longer a mere sublime abstraction) is seen from one view-point deified, from another incarnate. It comes to you, in Him, not only to command but to embrace. It is personified in Him who is at once infinitely the Righteous, and also the Propitiation for your sins.*
You hear of "claims," the claims of the Maker upon His work, of the Cause upon His effect. It is well,

---

* 1 John iii. 2.

but it is dark; it is cold, with the cold of mountain summits beneath the stars; but you find that those claims are the claims of the Lamb that was slain— they are the claims of the Man of Sorrows. Their Bearer has a heart, and a heart that was broken— "for us men and for our salvation." He comes indeed to say to you, with unfaltering and unreserved absoluteness, meaning every syllable as He says it, that you are not your own. His hand opens itself to clasp, to grasp, to use the being which He bought so dear. And it is a hand awful with omnipotence; it might crush what it holds even into annihilation. But behold the face, and in it see the will, the love, the heart! To that heart belongs that hand, and you know, as you surrender yourself to its divine tenacity, that it will hold you solely for purposes which are good and beautiful in the sight of a wisdom which is only the all-seeing eyes of a love which eternally passes knowledge, even the knowledge of the human heart.

Holy Fénelon, in the twenty-second of his "Reflections for a Month," quoting and commenting on a verse of Ecclesiasticus, "How great is the loving kindness of the Lord our God, and His compassion unto such as turn unto Him,"* writes thus: "Why do we delay to cast ourselves into the depth of this

* Ecclus. xvii. 29.

abyss? The more we lose ourselves therein, in faith and love, the safer we are. Let us give ourselves up to God without reserve or apprehension of danger. He will love us, and make us to love Him, and that love, increasing daily, shall produce in us all other virtues. He alone shall fill our heart, which the world has agitated and intoxicated, but could never fill; He will take nothing from us but what makes us unhappy; He will alter perhaps little in our actions" (leaving, he doubtless means, the path of daily duty unaltered externally), "and only correct the motive of them by making them all to be referred to Himself. Then the most ordinary and seemingly indifferent doings shall become exercises of virtue, sources of consolation. Then we shall cheerfully behold death approach as the beginning of life immortal, and, as St. Paul speaks, 'We shall not be unclothed but clothed upon, that mortality may be swallowed up of life.'"

Even so. The claim is infinitely right. The Claiment is the Lord who died for you and rose again; who loved you and gave Himself for you; whose insistence upon your surrender is but the issue of an affection infinitely wonderful and full of eternal promises. Wherefore, without a fear—for nothing is more safe, more happy, as nothing is more right—"present yourselves unto God, as those who are alive from the dead."* Assent and consent, at the feet of Jesus Christ, or rather, upon His heart, to the fact that "we are not our own."

I speak to-day in this honored place to some who are at the threshold of their Cambridge life. You are just touching the verge of those three years or so of early manhood which are like no other years, whose imprint must be left on all after-time for gain or loss—perhaps for glorious gain, perhaps for fatal loss. My friends and brethren, we who have known and loved Cambridge for years and years, bid our welcome to every new generation with an always deepening emotion. We know more and more, as we live here, what, for those who join us, for those who will soon succeed us, this place can be, in its double grandeur as a school of learning and a school of life. And in order that you may get not less out of Cambridge, but more; that you may reap the heaviest and the richest harvest, social, intellectual and moral, from the field you are free of now; that you may *be* to the utmost and *know* to the utmost and to the utmost be capacitated here, in the sense of all that is true and wholesome and of good report and serviceable to your generation—we beseech you to remember the fact that you are not your own. I am not here to deliver a studied homily upon either

* Rom. vi. 13.

the perils or the splendid opportunities of University life; but I am here to appeal, in my Lord's name, and as man to men, to any who shall care to listen; to appeal to them to be sure that, alike for strength and safety, for purity and pleasure, for real work and real rest, for luminous and wholesome insight into all true knowledge, for the opening of the largest and deepest sympathies between heart and heart, there is no secret like the daily, the hourly, recognition of the fact, "I am not my own."

The directions and applications of it will vary indefinitely, of course, with your varieties of character, calling and surroundings. To the man of social gift or aptitude, in whatever form, it will be a continual reminder, delicate but intense in its persistency, on the one hand, not to let his hours drift and perish in gregarious idleness; on the other, to understand that the golden talent of the faculty of attraction and contact can be used every day by your Lord, if you remember that you are never, anywhere, your own.

The man conscious that mind is strong within him by the gift of God, resolved for his part to maintain the great studious traditions of this place, in whatever walk of knowledge and thought, will find in his assent to the ownership of Jesus Christ not only the guidance and the caution, but the stimulus and, if I may so say, the clarification, of his intellectual powers. You belong to Him Who is Himself the primal Wisdom, whose "delights were" (and are) "with the sons of men."* "In Him are hid all the treasures of knowledge;" "In Him all things," visible, invisible, material, mental, spiritual, "consist."† In Jesus Christ is space enough for the whole sphere of knowledge to revolve, with all its constellations. They who learn and who think "in Him," shall indeed find, with Newton, with Sedgwick, with Adams, Lightfoot, Maxwell, Babington, that to serve Him is at once security and perfect freedom, in the world of mind as in the world of soul.

The man who sees himself, as he thinks, entrusted with one talent only (perhaps he hardly dares number even one), will find in the recognized fact that he belongs to Jesus Christ, the gold of heaven, already transmuting everything into itself. "The common round, the daily task," met in Jesus Christ; the trust faithfully fulfilled, for His sake; the not quite congenial study loyally pursued as duty; the life of self-respectful habit; the unobtrusive but distinct line of Christian obedience; the modest, cheerful, reverent confession of the Redeemer's name—here is an ideal which the man who just

* Prov. viii. 31. † Col. i. 10.

knows he is not his own, but that Christ is his, may realize every hour. And surely, so Scripture indicates,* it is over lives like these that the heavenly principalities bend with wonder, looking to see "the manifold wisdom of God" worked out in our mortal state.

And the man who glows with love, perhaps with newborn love, to Him who has saved him, let me say one word more to him about this life controlled and quickened by the watchword, "Not your own." The holy recollection will always animate you in your spiritual activities. You will be impelled by it to pray, and to watch, and to act, so that other lives may find what you have found, or what, rather, has found you. But your watchword will always chasten you and control you. The same power which keeps always burning the altar-fire of sacred love will quench the false flames of a zeal that forgets humility, an energy that despises loyalty, an enthusiasm that neglects duty. It will impel you in the line, not of least resistance but of most fidelity; it will consecrate for you the rule of discipline; it will glorify for you, with the will of God, your intellectual labor, and its results; it will make the class-list and the degree important to you with an ambition pure with the thought of God and of His will. Not

* Eph. iii. 10.

to protect self, not to spare it, but because precisely you are not your own, you will "exercise yourselves" in the plainest and most prosaic obligations, in those which on the mere surface may seem the least spiritual of all, "to have always a conscience void of offense both towards God and towards man."

Happy the life here which takes definitely the motto "I belong—I am not my own;" happy till over its grave at length is written the apostolic epitaph: "Having served his own generation by the will of God, he fell asleep." That last word cannot be uttered today without one reverent tribute to the illustrious name* just transferred from our academical registers to the long roll of the departed. Eminent, renowned, as a great medical man, consummate in the practice of his noble profession, a genuine scientific inquirer and discoverer, a master of wide and manifold knowledge, a teacher of the first order, a leader gifted with that enviable class of genius which knows how to call up, almost to create, the energies of others for the highest ends, brilliant in discourse and conversation, most excellent as a friend, Humphry, to the still youthful end of his long life, was emphatically one who "served his own generation," seeking, assuredly, to serve it

* Professor Sir George Murray Humphry, M.D., F.R.S., died Sept. 24, 1896.

"by the will of God." And, quite apart from his public energies, no one, I suppose, will ever know all the unobtrusive and generous good he did behind them—all the kindness, all the painstaking sympathy, all the bounty where he heard of need. Poor enough is this eulogy; but it was impossible not to pronounce it over the grave of one whose name and form have been so familiar, so conspicuous here, through much more than all my own Cambridge life τὸ γὰρ γέρας ἐστὶ θανόντων.

Meantime ours is still the pathway, not yet the goal. And for us, in the name of our Redeemer, along the pathway and for the goal, the inmost watchword must still be this, "Ye are not your own."

V

SELF-SURRENDER AND ITS POSSES-SIONS—II

Preached in the University Church, Cambridge

"Ye are not your own."—1 Cor. vi. 19.
"All things are yours."—1 Cor. iii. 21.

We gave our thoughts last Sunday to the former limb of this double text. Nearly from first to last we were occupied with "Ye are not your own," that watchword of obligation, that oracle of surrender. It claims for our Lord Jesus Christ nothing less than ourselves; it invades the very center of the life, and proclaims not the surroundings and the conditions only, but the man, to be the property of the Redeemer. "I belong, henceforth, not unto myself, but unto Him who died for me and rose again."

We took note already last week of another side of things. We remembered that under the strictness and exigency of "not your own" there lies latent a glorious world of liberty and life, the life of God in man. This comes powerfully out in the context of 1 Cor. vi. What are the words which just precede the "Ye are not your own"? They are the assurance to the Christian that "his body is the temple of the Holy Ghost, which he has of God;" that he "is joined unto the Lord, one spirit." He is property indeed, in a sense the most practical and prosaic; he is "bought, with a price." For St. Paul, no words are too plain to urge that thought home. He knows none of the dread felt by some theologians of what they are pleased to call a commercial Gospel. "Bought," "bought with a price," "bought out from the curse of the law," "purchased with His own blood"—such phrases, as you all know, lie at the very heart of the Pauline message. But then, they are vivified and glorified by the other elements of it. The being is possessed as property; but he is also possessed as living limb. Not only are his Lord's rights over him; his Lord's life is in him. Not only is he infinitely bound to do his Redeemer's will; he is so related to his Redeemer that he is wonderfully empowered to do it; and his law of liberty is just this—to do His will.

One pause of thought more before we leave last Sunday's special theme, and take up the second message of our text. The pause is for a reason perfectly practical. I stay to remind you *why* just there, in that close of 1 Cor. vi., St. Paul says that "you are not your own." He is not talking into the air. He has a human heart in view. He is reminding a desperately tempted man in old Corinth—Corinth with its worldly glitter and its seething vice—how not to sin. There is the Corinthian convert—the recent convert. His heathen heredity is in him, his old bad associations are around him. Is it possible for that man not to sin, not to fall, not to slide back into the mire again, and float down the black river? Yes, it is. But how? Not, in the judgment of the Apostle, by any *mere* inculcation of "you ought" and "you ought not;" not by any *mere* words, however they may burn, upon the shame of wrong and the eternal duty and beauty of right, of purity; no, but by the applied power of God. It can be done, by throwing at once into the very will and soul all the force, all the weight, all the life, of the inmost and most astonishing Gospel. It can be done, "in the name of the Lord Jesus, and by the Spirit of our God." So he tells the sinful man, in the thick of temptation, that he, having fled to Christ, is one with Christ; he is "one spirit" with Christ; his very body is "the temple" of the Holy One; he "is joined to the Lord."* Let him say all this to himself, as fact. Let him say all this to the tempter, to his face, as fact. So the tempted one shall "do valiantly," and only so. He is weak indeed; but his Lord is present with him, is dwelling in him, in

* 1 Cor. vi. 17.

every sense is in possession of him; and HE "shall tread down our enemies." In this war the Ark *must* be in the battle, and nothing less than the Ark. Jesus Christ Himself—for you, in you—must be your victory, your triumph against the devil, the world and the flesh.

> "Not me the dark foe fears at all,
> But hid in Thee I take the field;
> Now at my feet the mighty fall,
> For Thou hast bid them yield."

But it is time to come direct to that second member of the text which I reserved for our particular thought today: "All things are yours." What does this mean?

It is worth our while first to recall something of what it does not mean. It does not mean license, the parody and libel of liberty. It does not mean selfishness, the mind which grasps or which withholds at the dictate of self-will; this is not possession, but theft; this, in its effect, is nothing but the hard bondage and poverty of the being. It does not mean, God knoweth, the faintest shadow of a slur over moral distinctions—the bad dream that you can be so spiritual as to be, even for one fraction of a moment, emancipated from conscience; the lying whisper that you shall not surely die of permitted sin, because Christ died for you.

It does not mean a relaxation of the divine rule

of self-sacrifice; let us be sure of this. It is not spoken in order to throw the halo of the Gospel over a life which, professing godliness, is yet secretly, perhaps almost unconsciously, making itself as comfortable as possible for its own sake. It is not spoken to help us to minimize the call to bear the cross, and to serve the Lord in others, while we multiply and magnify excuses for indulgences and enjoyments which, however cultivated and refined, terminate in ourselves. The words are not given us to insinuate that, if we will but say "Lord, Lord," with a certain fervor, we may live as those who think that a man's "life" does "consist in the abundance of the things which he possesseth."

No, it cannot be so; we know that it cannot be. The whole Law, and the whole Gospel, both look the other way. They both equally belie reasonings from "All things are yours" which only mean the life of self come back again to the house left "empty, swept and garnished." The solemn context of the text is itself a warning. For what has gone just before? See verse 17, for the stern menace that "if any man defile the temple of God"—that is, himself—"him shall God destroy;" see verse 13, for the prophecy of the day of fire, when "every man's work shall be tested, of what sort it is." And verse 18 conveys the entreaty not to be deceived by a specious wisdom which prefers the world to God.

But then, most certainly, the words have a meaning, positive and beautiful—"All things are yours." They are spoken indeed to those, and to those only, who are not their own, but their Lord's possession. But they do not merely restate that side of truth. They give its contrast and its complement. They turn the shield quite round, to show its other face— and it *is* another. "You are not your own"—be sure of that; it is an immovable fact. "All things are yours"—be sure of that also; it is meant to carry to you a magnificent message, affirmative, distinctive, altogether its own.

For explanation and application, let us look first at the near context, and read the short section comprised in verses 21 to 23: "Let no man glory in man. For all things are yours; whether Paul, or Apollos, or Cephas, or the world, or life, or death, or things present, or things to come, all are yours; and ye are Christ's and Christ is God's." Here is the occasion here is the reason of the words. The Corinthians, you remember, had been forgetting in a particular way the grandeur of their direct, immediate, spiritual relation to God in Christ. They had lost sight in one quarter of what it was to be *His own*. They had been attaching themselves to human leaders, as such, in a way which obscured their own wonderful connection with the Eternal Love. They had given themselves over to a party spirit, a divided and vehement partisanship, which befitted rather the tools of rival chiefs in a secular struggle than those for whom even Apostles and Prophets existed as only servants of the saints of God. Now, above this miserable trouble they were to rise, in the recollection of the fact that, because God in Christ had annexed them directly to Himself, God in Christ was directly concerned to make everything combine for their fullest and most perfect good. They were not a set of cliques; they were the Family of God. Then they had something better to do than to support or to acclaim a leader and lift him upon a pedestal. If he was indeed a man sent from God, he was given to them, not they to him. Taken as believers, they all were the children for whom their Father would do anything. Taken as a messenger, even an Apostle was but a servant, ordered to do his uttermost for them. Were they the Lord's, given to Him, with all they had? Then, by the law of divine relation, the Lord, with all He had, was theirs, given to them. And He had all things. So all things, being His, were theirs.

We have here at once a fact full of grace and

glory. And it is lifted far above place and time. Now as then, now and for ever, the man who belongs to Christ in truth, assenting from the soul to the ownership of his Redeemer, is out and out His property. But he is also, and at the same moment, and with equal reality, His brother. In that deep and inmost sense of the terms on which Scripture dwells with inexhaustible and loving recurrence, he is "a child of God." And his Father will do anything for him. Nothing of his Father's resources shall be grudged to him. Wisdom and love may, and will, sort and sift, and in that sense limit the things which shall be put actually into the child's hands. But the whole wealth of the great home is his, in the sense that he is the child for whom anything shall be done. On him no resources are too great to spend. His utmost good is watched for, always and everywhere. His Father delights exceedingly to meet his wishes, and limits the meeting of them only by the interests of the child; and He has made those interests identical with His own.

Is not this a thought, let me rather say a fact, with which every Christian man is to look around and find life transfigured? "My Lord, my Father, I am ever with Thee, and all that Thou hast is mine. Thou hast put much actually into my hands, out of Thy treasuries. I have but to open my eyes and count a few of Thy blessings, and they begin to crowd and multiply upon my view. But behind them lies the immeasurable wealth always latent in the fact that Thou art mine, that Thou art devoted to me. Not in dream or poem, but in 'a sober certainty of waking bliss,' I may confidently say this. Thou art devoted to me. Giver of Thine own Son, wilt Thou not, dost Thou not, with Him also freely give me all things?* All is mine; some of the all is in my hands, the rest in trust with Thee."

Adolphe Monod, great saint, great teacher, great sufferer, lying on a premature couch of anguish and death, forty years ago, at Paris, collected in his bed-chamber, Sunday by Sunday, a little congregation of friends; Guizot was sometimes of the number. There he addressed them, like Standfast in the Pilgrim's Progress, as from the very waters of the last river, speaking always on his lifelong theme, Jesus Christ. The pathetic series of these *Adieux a ses Amis et a l'Eglise* was gathered after his death into a volume. Late in its pages comes a discourse with the title, *All in Jesus Christ*. From this let me quote a few sentences; they deal with our theme of this afternoon: "Be it wisdom, be it light, be it power, be it victory over sin, be it a matter of this world or of the world to come, all is in Christ. Having Christ, we have all

* Rom. viii. 32.

things; bereft of Christ, we have alsolutely nothing. 'All things are yours, and you are Christ's, and Christ is God's.' Well, then, what is the result for me? I am poor, it may be. Yet all the fortunes of this world are mine; for they are Christ's, who Himself is God's, and who could easily give them all to me, with Himself, if they would serve my interests. The whole world, with all its glories, with all its power, belongs to me; for it belongs to my Father, who will give it me to-morrow, and could give it me to-day, if that were good for me. I am very ill, it may be. Yet health is mine, strength is mine, comfort is mine, a perfect enjoyment of all the blessings of life is mine; for all this belongs to Christ, who belongs to God, and who disposes of it as He will. If He withholds these things from me to-day, for a fleeting moment, swift as the shuttle in the loom, it is for reasons wholly of His own; it is because these pains and this bitterness conceal a benediction worth more to me than the health so precious, than the comfort so delightful. . . . I challenge you to find a thing of which I cannot say: 'This is my Father's; therefore it is mine; if He withholds it to-day, He will give it me to-morrow.' I trust myself to His love. All is mine, if I am His."

Let us, too, with the saintly Parisian pastor, look at life, at real life, from this transcendent yet absolutely practical point of view. There is another side of the message, as we will presently remember. There is wonderfully opened to you in Jesus Christ a secret of intense enjoyment, a delightful sense of possession, for the sunny fields and morning hours of life. But you will approach that fact the better for a firm recollection first, that life is not all sunshine; and that is by no means your first business to make it as comfortable as you can for yourself, but to "gird up the loins of your mind" to do and to bear and to "hope to the end;"* and then that over life *thus* considered the Lord can cast the glory of the fact that in Him all things are yours. In Him you possess the dominate circumstance; you are not its victim but its employer. In Him, in the ultimate truth of the matter, you are lifted out of disappointment and its power. You may seem to sink, to faint, to fail; you may wear out; you may be thrown aside; your "purposes," as *you* see them, may be "broken off." But are you Christ's? Are you a limb of His body? Are you the willing implement of His will? Then you are being somehow manipulated and used by One who eternally succeeds, and you, too, are successful so. It was thus that St. Paul himself, in his last prison, was able to dictate the words: "Nevertheless I am not ashamed;"† I

* 1 Pet. i. 13. † 2 Tim. i. 12.

am not disappointed. From other points of sight than this he might well be a disappointed man. Taken apart from Christ, he was failing amidst a whole world of failures; it *looked as if* his life's work were being wrecked and extinguished by the tremendous world-power, awakened to fear and anger; his teaching was travestied or discredited in the Church; his heart's affections were lacerated; himself by all men was forsaken. But he "knew whom he had believed." He was in the hands of Jesus Christ, and he knew it. And there he was invulnerable to disappointment, in his all-seeing and all-controlling Lord.

It is only when you are really armed in Christ for the shocks and storms of life that you are really safe to remember that you are enabled in Christ for a double enjoyment of its joys. But now, it is even so —you are so enabled. I dare with confidence to affirm that the Christian believer, surrendered to his Lord and at rest in Him, is, in a sense perfectly human, however much it is also divine, the happiest, the most cheerful man. This is natural; it is as it should be. It is for him alone that Humanity wears all its greatness and Nature shines with all her glory. More and more, as the world rolls on and human insight grows with watching, a pervading melancholy threatens the heart which observes and tastes, but is not in Jesus Christ. For what is there, out of Him, and away from the certainties in Him of a life eternal, which is not already touched by the shadows of an ultimate and illimitable death? But in Christ you see man redeemed, and man's life invested in Him with a boundless present interest, and with possibilities "unspeakable and full of glory." In Christ, the Cause and Keystone of creation,* man sees the Universe at last warm and living with a Soul. He loves the Artificer in the Work; he understands and feels the Heart within the Vesture.† To him the events of the day are pregnant with the providence of his Father and of his eternal Brother, and this gives them at once a dignity and a hope unknown elsewhere. To him the mountain and the forest, the flood and the cloud, are the work, the characteristic handiwork, of his inmost Friend. In Cowper's words, in the "Task," in a passage of the highest order, he

> "Acknowledges with joy
> His manner, and with rapture tastes his style."

To him the largest incidents of his path and also the smallest, are not only things to be somehow met; they are touches and pressures of the Hand which manages everything "for good to them that love God." He can deal with things so seen as more

* See Ps. cii. 26.   † See Col. i. 16, 17.

than a spectator. He is a son and heir upon his Father's property. He is concerned; he possesses; he is at home.

That is a noble sentence in the "Apology" of Aristides (Chap. xvi.), where the observer of the Church describes the cheerfulness of primitive Christian life, and, let us add, of primitive Christian death. "As men who know God," he writes, "they ask of Him petitions which are proper for Him to give and for them to receive; and they thus accomplish the course of their lives. And because they acknowledge the goodnesses of God towards them—lo! for them there flows forth the beauty that is in the world."

"Never," said a thoughtful young Cambridge man of a recent generation, "never, till I knew my Lord indeed, did I really see the beauty of branch and foliage in the trees." Yes, Jesus Christ can restore the loss mourned by the great poet; He can more than "bring us back the hour of splendor in the grass, of glory in the flower." In the Eastern wildernesses a beloved friend of my own,* a missionary of the Cross in the most difficult of fields, a man whose inmost instincts ask for the cultured and the beautiful (and, as to human arts, ask this now in vain), has found God wonderfully present to him in Nature

* The Rev. H. Carless, M.A., of Corpus Christi College. He died in the province of Kerman, in Persia, 1898.

—cheering, uplifting, giving company. The constellations of the Persian midnight have been alive to him with the smile of his Master. The solitary tree upon the hill, the tuft of flowers beside the upland track, have taken on them for his eyes a beauty as of Paradise; the thought of God in them has responded to the life of God in him.

> "Heaven above is softer blue,
>   Earth around is sweeter green;
> Something lives in every hue
>   Christless eyes had never seen."

"All things are yours; whether things present or things to come." The one region is yours as truly as the other. To-day is yours; your "to-day," young man, with all its interests, its force, its hopes, with all its contents and development; every step of all the path—ay! till it enters that eternal future which already casts its solemn radiance upon to-day. "All things are yours, whether life or death." Life is yours, to enjoy heartily, to understand profoundly, to use as your precious possession; for you are its owner, for you are a child of God. And then, death is yours. Wonderful words!—but so they stand, a paradox of blessing. How much it looks as if we rather were death's prey! But in Christ the veil is lifted, and death is found to be the possession of His servant. The thing may come soon or come late. It may advance slowly upon you, and in full view; it may strike you from an ambush, and in the twinkling of an eye, as only last Tuesday, in our midst, it struck an honored life,* and bade us (so soon again after our last bereavement)† lament another work cut short, another circle of many friendships broken, another heart left desolate. Yet death in Christ, O Christian man, is yours. It is not an accident; it is a gift. It is not a spectre, hideous with the relics of the sepulchre; it is the Angel of the Presence, stepping from within the eternal tent‡ to lift its curtain for the believer's entrance in. It is the "silent opener of" that "gate" as to the other side of which we have just this revealed,§ that while life for Christ is real, is happy, is rich, is free, is immeasurably good, "to depart and to be with Christ is far, far better" still.

*The Rev. F. Pattrick, Tutor of Magdalene College, died very suddenly, October 6, 1896.
† See above, p. 46.
‡ See Luke xvi. 9.   § Phil. i, 23.

VI.

THE SELF-CONSECRATION OF THE CHRIST

Preached on Christmas Day, in the University Church, Cambridge.

"Then said He, Lo, I have come to do Thy will, O God."—HEB. x. 9.

"Then said I, Lo, I have come; I delight to do Thy will."—Ps. xl. 7, 8.

I INVITE you this Christmas afternoon to a *sursum corda*. *Habeamus ad Dominum;* "Let us hold our hearts up unto the Lord;" let us kneel in recollecting faith at the cradle of the Incarnation; and let us look up from beside it to the heaven of heavens, to ponder a little while that great antecedent to Bethlehem, the Self-Consecration of the Eternal Son to His incarnate life and work.

This lies here before us in the Scriptures of the text, in the New Testament and in the Old. What was the immediate occasion and impulse to the writing of Psalm xl. I do not ask; no certain answer is even remotely possible. But for all who accept without reserve the interpreting authority of the apostolic Scriptures, it is settled by Hebrews x. that the ultimate purpose of Him who moved the Psalmist to write was to reveal to us the thought and intent of the Christ Himself, in His will to come into the world.

The consciousness of the Psalmist may have been this, or it may have been that, as he took up his harp and sung his wonderful song of joy and conflict. There is nothing to entitle us to assert, as if we knew, that his condition was not purely and directly prophetic; that he did not sing in a rapture of the Spirit, in a state of holy second sight, easily overleaping sense and time. On the other hand there is nothing to entitle us to assert, as if we knew, that such a rapture was then and there upon him. But this we may affirm, if the witness of the Christian Scriptures is adequate for us, that the Psalmist's Inspirer, moving him to utter what he did, meant, ultimately, to speak an oracle concerning the King Eternal, the Christ of God. So the Scripture, with both its hands, the prophetic and the apostolic, lifts for us here the veil from no less a secret than this. It discloses to us "the mind that was in Christ Jesus," when, in the eternity which is above our time, He, the Son with the Father, the Son of the Father's love, the Son "beloved before the foundation of the universe," willed to come down and to become flesh. It utters to us the thought

SELF-CONSECRATION OF CHRIST.

with which He, being true God, elected to be also true Man. It lets us hear His resolve to come and to do the Father's will, in saving us.

> "There, on the heights of primal Deity,
> Before all worlds, Messiah will'd to part
> Himself from glory, and in destined time
> So parted, for us men, descending thence
> With voice of consecration, 'Lo, I come
> To do Thy will.'"

How shall we think aright, how shall we speak, of such a thing? Here is a theme, if any, to make us remember the vanity of words without the Spirit, the paltriness of the tinkling of speech where the Lord of love does not give and guide the message. But may He, in His great mercy, not leave us alone with this matter. Then, and only then, something may be attained by our thought which shall indeed be His.

Now, what have we in the whole Book of God more wonderful in its kind than this revelation, given us through the Epistle and the Psalm? It comes with all the holy simplicity characteristic of Scripture. Nothing is intruded here of that imaginative or rather fanciful detail with which even a Milton can only spoil the theme of the counsels of Heaven:

> "In quibbles angel and archangel join,
> And God the Father turns a school divine."

All is brief and unrestrained, but all is wonderful. We are suffered to overhear eternal Voices speaking to one another upon the Throne. By implication, we hear One call, as if looking for agency and messenger: "Whom shall I send? Who will go?" And then from a height no lower, from a glory no less excellent, Another answers: "Lo, I have come!" The answer sounds in the tone of nothing less than Godhead; for it is the utterance of an absolute freewill, issuing in action of absolute wonderfulness and merit. But it is an answer also in the tone of subordination: it gives and yields, it speaks a personal surrender to a personal disposal. He who here "comes to do a will" in some sense not His own, is immeasurably free of exterior constraints to submission. But He submits. And in His submission a divine moral fitness strikes perfect harmony with a divine moral freedom.

What shall we say of the words "O God, *O my God,*" heard as we listen at the sanctuary door? Can it be that even before Incarnation the Coming One could thus address the Sender? Is the eternal Subordination of the Son a warrant for such a thought, under the safeguard of a full concurrent confession of our Redeemer's proper Godhead? It is hard to put the thought into form without running into inferences, or at least associations, which touch the border of Christian orthodoxy, if they do not cross it. Perhaps we may rather see in the words an anticipation, a wonderful *prolepsis,* in the divine thought of the Speaker. That thought is consistent. He says not "I go," but "*I come,*" or more literally, in the Hebrew, "*I have come,*" as one who is already in the region to which He wills to descend. In the same sense, surely, He says "O my God," as if He had already taken on Him the nature in which He was to be able to say, "We know what *we worship,*"* and to cry "Eli, Eli" from the Cross. It is the Son, submitting and self-consecrating, even upon the throne. It is God the Son of God, giving there this infinite example of the glory of a holy surrender and service, illustrating with the light unapproachable the bliss and perfect freedom of a true *Thy will be done.*

Many an echo from earth has answered that heavenly Voice. One after another, sinful men in their great need have come to the Son of God, to be accepted by Him and united to Him. They have been made one with Him in the double union of righteousness and of life. They have received His merit, the justification which the "Head, once wounded," wrought out for the members. But also they have been filled with His Spirit, the Spirit of

* John iv. 24.

the SON, "which they that believe on Him receive" out of His immeasurable fulness. And in the power of that uniting and possessing Spirit they have found, in their complete weakness, capacity to tread, in measure, in His steps. Many a human heart in receiving Christ has experienced as fact what seemed once an incredible, or even a repellent, dream, that it is good to be not our own. It has discovered the blessedness of an unreserved submission, and obedience, and servitude to the will of God; the sober truth of the old confession, *Tibi servire est regnare;* the strange but genuine joy involved and conveyed in the full acceptance of that rule of life given us by the Apostle, "Whether we live, we live unto the Lord; and whether we die, we die unto the Lord; whether we live therefore or die, we die unto the Lord; whether we live therefore or die, we are the Lord's."* Tersteegen's hymn, "O allersusste Gottesville," gives utterance not to his own soul only, but to innumerable others of the past and of this hour:

> "Thou sweet, beloved Will of God,
>   My anchor-ground, my fortress-hill,
> My spirit's silent fair abode—
>   In thee I hide me, and am still."

Fénelon's dying whisper, summing up his life,

* Rom. xiv. 8.

Fiat voluntas tua, is not his only, but that of all true disciples. Guyon's assurance is as good for us as it was for her two centuries ago:

> "Yield to the Lord with simple heart,
> All that thou hast and all thou art;
> Renounce all strength but strength divine,
> And peace shall be for ever thine."

But these inmost spiritual joys of the Christian, born out of the depth of a true surrender to the will of God, are not original, but derived. They are all descendants, and, as it were, reverberations of that divine and primal joy of the Son when He said, on the throne, in view of His descent: "Lo, I have come, to do Thy will, O My God; I am content to do it; yea, Thy law is within My heart."

It is a thing indeed for wonder and for worship, to see here the law of holiness and happiness for the disciple found first in its glorious idea within the Godhead itself. The eternal relations of the Holy Trinity make the archetype of all created goodness. Within that secret place where the One is Three and the Three are One, the bliss, the μακαριότης,* of Godhead, includes the blessedness of surrender; "I delight to do Thy will."

As we listen from below to this heavenly colloquy of sending and of submission, the Apostle stands beside us, with his Philippian Letter, and bids us

* 1 Tim. i. 2.

read its message, and there learn in solemn detail what this, "Lo, I come," was to be for Him who uttered it. We open his second chapter, and we read how "Christ Jesus looked not upon His own things, but upon the things of others." "Being as He was in the form of God"—ἐν μορφῇ Θεοῦ ὑπάρχων—in the reality and glory of the Eternal Nature, "He counted it not a plunderer's spoil, His equality with God;" He did not deal with that supreme and rightful Dignity as a thing to be used jealousy and for Himself. "He made Himself void, by taking on Him Form of Bondservant." — ἐκένωσεν ἑαυτὸν, μορφὴν δούλου λαβών. He entered upon the conditions and experience of human bond-service. He stooped under the yoke of that absolute and obligatory service to the Heavenly Father which is due from the created nature. He came to *be* Man, and also to *seem* Man— ἐν ὁμοιώματι ἀνθρώπων γενόμενος —to be Man, undisguised and open. And, so being, "He obeyed," and still obeyed. He carried out the consecration uttered in heaven into all the humble and all the awful experiences of manhood and of earth. He obeyed— μέχρι θανάτου —"to the length of death;" the final submission was rendered when "He hid not His face from shame and spitting," and stretched forth His hands, and "made His soul an offering for sin," and died "the death of the Cross."

SELF-CONSECRATION OF CHRIST.   103

Let our Christmas contemplation send us to weigh again that familiar but inexhaustible paragraph of the Philippians. We have heard the fortieth Psalm; it gives us the purpose of the obedient Redeemer, as it was spoken out in the heaven of heavens. St. Paul in the message to Philippi gives us that also. But he goes on instantly to dilate on the Lord's *action upon His purpose.* He leads us to see Him in His historical assumption of our nature, as He took it on Him, and with it all its essential relations to the claims of God. He calls us to watch Him walking with men as the Servant of God, till He walks at length, in the path of an absolute surrender, to the encounter with human sin, to the bearing of human guilt, to the endurance of the divine sentence—to the shame, the horror, the agony, of "the accursed Tree."

And St. Paul, more explicitly than the Psalm, as was fitting, reminds us how the great Consecrator of Himself to the Father's will thought all the while of man as well as of God. True, the inmost and ruling intention of that wonderful obedience was the doing of the Father's will as such, the glorification of the Father in the doing of His will. But the context and argument of the Apostle remind us that, under that supreme intention, the thought of "us men and our salvation" was as perfectly present to the exalted Christ as if there had been nothing else to think of upon the throne. For how does St. Paul come, in Philippians ii., to speak of the self-surrender of the Son at all? It is for a purpose as human and as practical as possible. It is to bring it home to the believer that *he* is to "look not upon his own things but upon the things of others." This the Apostle presses home upon the souls of his converts, in the true manner of the Gospel, not by an ethical abstract, but by the glorious Christian concrete—by the motive of the love and of the work of Christ.

To look upon the things of others—this, he would have us to understand, as far as ever we can understand it—this was what Christ Jesus did when He dealt as He did with His "Equality," and took on Him the nature in which He was to serve the will of God, even unto death. He was thinking all the while of us. He looked upon our things. He cared—oh, how greatly did He care!—for us.

I have heard it said of that true scholar and most faithful servant of God, the late Professor Scholefield, whom I still see and hear in his pulpit, as one of the memories of my childhood, that worshipers in his Church of St. Michael, in this town, observed that he never could get through the Nicene Creed, at the Holy Table, without an audible faltering of the

SELF-CONSECRATION OF CHRIST. 105

voice when he recited the words, "Who for us men and for our salvation came down from heaven." Scholefield was by no means a man of effusive and demonstrative emotions. His manner was, in fact, on common occasions, somewhat reserved and cold. But he lived near his Lord. He was one who, amidst the necessary publicities of his duty, spent much time alone with Him, meditating closely and deeply upon redeeming love. And so he entered into something of the hidden depth of his Master's heart and the hidden meaning of this wonderful, "Lo, I have come," this "taking of the Bondservant's Form."

As we stand listening to the voice which thus, even from the divine glory, speaks of surrender and of service, let us take up the Scriptures once more, and recall in shortest summary some of the truths told us by the way through this utterance, "Lo I have come to do Thy will."

i. First, the saying, taken in its context, speaks of the exalted place which the sacrificial and atoning Work of our Lord in death holds in the plan of Redemption. The Psalm, interpreted by the Epistle to the Hebrews, puts this into sacred prominence. "I have come." So speaks the eternal Christ in view of the mystery of His Incarnation; "I have come." As if to say that He is already on the march, already in the work, already taking genuine Manhood of a mortal Mother, so that the two Natures, whole and perfect, never to be confused, never to be divided, shall meet in ineffable union under one Person, one Christ, that He may be, and may work, in them both. But *why* does He come, as to the immediate and urgent element of the purpose? What is the aim set *in the foreground* of the eternal thought, indicated in the Psalm and developed in the Epistle? Is it, immediately, to knit up mankind together into one? Is it, immediately, to redeem the race by Incarnation? It is, immediately, to be "Sacrifice and Offering." It is to do at last the work which the altar, under the old law, could never do. It is that the Incarnate, being such, "might put away sins by the sacrifice of Himself." Such was the first ruling purpose of the Self-Consecration of the Son. The Self-Consecrator had in view, above all things, His Death, His Sacrifice, His Expiation, His Propitiation. Psalm, and Hebrews, and Philippians, all, in this matter, gravitate upon the Crucifixion. "A body hast Thou prepared Me." "He took share and share, with His brethren, in flesh and blood, that by *means of death* He might destroy him that had the power of death." "Being the brightness of the Father's glory, by Himself he *purged our sins.*" "He became obedient, even to the length of the death of the Cross."

ii. Secondly, our Scriptures are eloquent of the pain and yet joy of the untold Humiliation of the Lord. They tell us of His willingness to be made like us, with a likeness that should be no trope or figure, but a reality to its depths. They reveal His divinely free consent, in the full light of God, to enter personally within the essential and sinless limitations of humanity. He willed, as Man, to experience what is meant by growth and by development, what it is to weep and to wonder, what it should be to say, "Thy will be done," not only in heaven, as the Son Eternal, but as the Son of Man, under the olives of Gethsemane. He willed to cry, when the last blackness gathered round the Cross, to Him whose will He was wholly content to do, "Why hast Thou forsaken Me?" He willed to commit the outgoing Human Spirit into His hands, in the awfulness of human death.

Are we to go further? Shall we say that He was then consenting also to other limitations? Was He committing Himself to such restrictions of intellectual and, we must add (for this cannot be wholly excluded), of moral insight, as would make it possible that He should share with His brethren not only their fatigues and sorrows, but their illusions and mistakes? Ἐκένωσεν ἑαυτὸν, says the Epistle; "He made Himself void." And the κένωσις, "the Exinanition," became an almost synonym with the Church Fathers for "the days of the flesh" of the humiliated Lord. "He was in truth and nature God," says the Alexandrian Cyril, "even before the times of the *Kenôsis;* and, again, "He became Man and humbled Himself into *Kenôsis.*" Now, did that *Kenôsis* actually imply, what certainly the Fathers little suspected it to do when they used the term, the submission of our Redeemer to share, as a Teacher, *the fallibility* of men? It is not willingly that I touch that supremely important problem. But its present prominence in Christian thought seems to forbid us, if we approach the region at all, quite to pass it by. Only two suggestions would I offer here, in much humility, but with a deep persuasion that the matter lies close to the vitals of the Faith.

For one thing, it would seem to be a grave mistake of thought, when we are dealing with a Humiliation undertaken for a supremely benignant end, accepted in order to the highest benefit of man, to class under its idea a voluntary, a foreseeing consent to be capable of mistakes, and so, inevitably, to be capable of leading others to be mistaken, too. To own that the Lord submitted, in a sublime surrender, to the necessities of weakness and of sorrow, and even that He abnegated awhile the consciousness and exercise of Omniscience—this is one thing. But it is a quite different thing when He is conceived to have consented *not to know,* as a Teacher, *that He did not know*—not to be aware whether He was or was not mistaken in whatever He claimed the right to say. Such a consent, if conceivable, would not be easy to explain as part of a benignant purpose, an element in a Humiliation divinely calculated for the illumination of man.

The passage before us, in the Psalm and the Epistle, seems to give intimations just to the contrary of the theory referred to. For it indicates to us, by its previous and its following context, that the Christ in His heavenly glory had already full in view the ancient Ritual, and descended at the Father's will not only to meet its inevitable defect, but *to fulfil its import,* as all true and all of God. What He thought of the old Order in the days of His flesh, what He then said and did about the Law and about the Prophets, was thus but the continuation of His thought about them upon the throne.

For another thing, if we seek the true Scriptural import of the *Kenôsis,* the Philippian passage (its original) must be consulted; and it seems to direct us in a line just opposite to that which would make fallibility an element in the Lord's Humiliation.

SELF-CONSECRATION OF CHRIST.

Ἐκένωσεν ἑαυτόν, μορφὴν δούλου λαβών. If we interpret the Greek phrase by well-recognized rule, we must take the verb and the participle as contributing to give us, from two sides, one fact. "He made Himself void," not anyhow, but *thus*—"taking Bond-servant's Form." The "Avoidance" was, in fact, just this—the "taking." It was the assumption of the creaturely Nature, the becoming, in Augustine's words, "Creature, as He was Man"— *quod ad Hominem, Creatura;* and the assumption of it in just this respect, that in it He became, by the fact of it, — Δοῦλος —Bond-servant. But what is the implication of that unique, absolute, unreserved, unhindered Bond-service of the Incarnate Son? What does it say to us in respect of His capacity to do the Father's work, and convey His mind, and deliver His message? The absoluteness of this subjection of the perfect BOND-SERVANT gives us warrant not of the precariousness but of the perfection of the conveyance of the SENDER's mind. *"He whom God hath sent speaketh the words of God."*

His own servant Paul was one day to claim authority as messenger just because of the intensity of his slavery. "Let no man trouble me, for I bear in my body the *stigmata* of the Master, Jesus" (Gal. vi. 17). The supreme Bond-servant, the Bearer of the *stigmata* of the cross, has right then, indeed, to claim our unreserved, our worshiping silence as He speaks. He, in perfect relation to His Sender, perfectly conveys His Sender's mind. He says nothing but what his sender bids Him say.

But let us turn from discussion, and end where we set out, in faith and in adoration, before the self-consecrating Saviour.

We are keeping the festival of joy. The splendor of God, once poured upon the field of the shepherds, shines for ever upon this day. The great carol of the warrior-angels, the choiring heavenly army, στρατιὰ οὐράνιος, sounds on for ever in our winter sky. For us men God is made Man:

> "Thou art my flesh and bone,
> Thou dost my kindred own,
> Thou Light of the eternal Morn;
> And sitting at Thy feet,
> I find it passing sweet
> To think that I too was of woman born."

But the roots of our Christian joy are watered with the sorrows and the sacrifices of our Redeemer. They cost him dear. They involved His infinite Humiliation. As we rejoice, let it be with that thought in our souls. Let us bless Him with the love of penitents; let us follow Him with the love of witnessing disciples. "Lo, I have come." So said the Son of God, in view of His Cradle and of His Cross, as

He saw them from above all the heavens. "Lo, I have come to do Thy will." And we are His. We are, through His grace, in Him. Then be it ours, this day, this Birthday, to say the like, in our little measure, as if we had never said it before, for His sake and in His name. For trial, for humiliation, for the death of self-will, for whatever may be for us the cross, let us, His members, draw from Him the power to say, "I have come," and to "delight to do the will of Him that sent us, and to finish His work."

VII
THE INDIVIDUAL AND GOD

Preached in the University Church, Cambridge

"But it is good for me to draw near to God."—Ps. lxxiii. 28.

"BUT as for me, approach to God, nearness to God, for me is good." So we may render the Psalmist's original words, with due attention to their emphasis upon the person of the speaker. Ἐμοὶ δὲ τὸ προσκολλᾶσθαι τῷ Θεῷ ἀγαθόν ἐστι: so reads the Septuagint. And the Vulgate follows: *Mihi autem adhaerere Deo bonum est.*

The whole stress of the sentence lies upon the individual and independent decision. Let other people, let the whole world, if it will, retire into a distance from God, and live apart and to themselves. *My* choice is made, definite, irrevocable, and, above all, my own. To approach God, to abide close to God, face to Face, spirit to Spirit, love to Love, person to Person—this for me is good. This is my *summum bonum,* nearness to Him.

I ask to address you this afternoon upon some relations of the individual to God in Christ, relations of spiritual access and intercourse. The theme is high, the ground is holy; let me remember and beware. But the matter is quite as practical as it is sacred; it is of the utmost consequence to the actual Christian life that we should think aright upon it, and put what we think into use. Moreover, the question is, if I do not greatly mistake, particularly timely to some exigencies of our time. Fashions of thought are largely abroad which call for a temperate but firm reassertion, now and again, of the individualistic aspect of the spiritual life; otherwise, even its collective interests will suffer loss.

Let me speak first upon this latter and less general topic; it will lead us directly on to what is more abiding and universal.

Who does not know, then, that strong and manifold drifts of opinion around us set towards all that is corporate and collective? They touch and draw us, like the secret currents of the ocean, in every kind of connection, social, civil, and religious. In religion the tendency is everywhere, in one mode of it or another. Here and there the teacher, numerously followed, lays his insistence upon collective "Humanity," as the object of Redemption, as the organ of Revelation. In Humanity he sees the developing manifestation of God, who inbreathes and informs it with His Spirit, and whose eternal Word is its Archetype and its Sum. The term sounds on perpetually through such teaching, like the theme of a fugue; we are occupied and impressed with the life and growth of Humanity, its liberation from evil, its education into advancing stages of good. The tendency is to apply to it the whole biblical vocabulary of salvation, from the first purpose of eternal mercy to the glory that is to be revealed.

"The Kingdom of God," again, is a term characteristic of whole types of influential thought; I need only name, for one, that of the school of Ritschl. It is a term wholly scriptural; its true significance therefore, of course, is altogether for the highest good. But the risk is, a use of it ruled not by Scripture but by speculation. As a fact, it has been used largely to promote conceptions of man's relation to God under which the individual sinks and is merged in "the Kingdom." He must seek his blessings, if he is to be blest, only as he lives in its life, only, if I may say so, through its large mediation.

In other quarters (though all these types of thought often cross each other's borders) the great word, *Church,* is made the resonant theme of all the music. No matter, for the moment, what definition in detail is given to the word; it denotes a sacred Society, corporate and collective. The idea of such an august entity fairly rules whole theologies, and meets us at all turns. So presented, the Church as such is the true object and recipient of salvation, the seer, the teacher, of its message. It is the avenue to Christ the shrine; the way to Christ, the end. Nay, rather, it, in its collectivity, is so joined to Him, so filled, so impregnated with Him, that we cannot as individuals touch Him with a sure touch except through it; scarcely, on the other hand, can we touch it without therefore touching Him.

So I have heard, with deep attention, devout expounders exhibit and enforce the theory. They repelled the suggestion that their doctrine gave prominence to the Church at the expense of the supreme prominence of her Lord. They contended that so has He given Himself to her, so has He, for our blessing, lodged Himself in her, that in her we have Him. It is difficult to say too much of the Church, just because of Jesus Christ.

Naturally, under such convictions the vocabulary of salvation tends to be applied prevalently to this great collective existence. The process of grace from eternity to eternity is largely viewed as taking place upon the Body rather than upon the member, or, however, upon the member only through the Body. Rather the Church than the soul, the man, is the primary object of promise and of gift.

The tendencies thus roughly indicated carry in them, every one, powerful elements of truth. Mere individualism, if it means the individual's isolation into self-sufficiency and self-will, is indeed a fatal fallacy. Alike for him and all that is about him, it is simply evil. As surely as the man was constituted not for himself but for God, so surely was he constituted not for himself but for others. So conscience intimates; so Revelation affirms. The Bible almost opens with the divine assertion that it is not good for the man to be alone. Its last veil falls upon the fair vision of a Society which is at once the Bride with her Husband and the City with its King. The history of Redemption develops all along the magnificent idea of a hallowed Community, related as such to God, receiving as such His blessings, strengthening itself by the fellowship of its members before Him, guarding His message of grace and hope, and commissioned to convey it to the world. "Glorious things are spoken" of the Church of Christ. In the Epistles the words labor with the effort to express its excellency. It is the Body of the exalted Head, the Organ for His operation. It is the Spouse, the Object of His divine complacency, and of the vast Sacrifice of His love, nourished and cherished, and, at last, glorified by Him. Race, and age, and rank, and sex, are all merged in this wonderful aggregate: "You are all one, one being, εἶς ἐστε, in Christ Jesus."*

* Gal. iii. 28.

The non-individual side of Christian life is indeed prominent in the Scriptures. It may be distorted, it may be travestied, but it is a vital fact. Men, the best of men, may attempt impossible definitions of the Church, but the Church is a mighty factor in the plan of God. Things quite unpractical may be said about cohesion and unity. They may be preached, in their most exterior aspects, as almost Alpha and Omega, as if collectivity of system were a more vital thing than the eternal truths which touch most directly the personal conscience and the personal will. Yet cohesion and unity are not only noble principles to entertain; they make altogether for our practical blessing, temperately understood. The dislocation of Christendom, the collision of Christians, can never, as such, be according to the mind of God.

So those watchwords, familiar in our day—"Church life," "Church work," "Corporate action"—are abundantly salutary in their place. They have a mission against the evils inseparable from a thoughtless or a self-willed isolation, reminding the individual that he cannot possibly live aright if he lives and works in a would-be spiritual life, related only to himself. Not only must his usefulness greatly suffer if he labors, ever so hard, quite outside constituted connection; his own spiritual interests, his own innermost man, must bear loss, if he

THE INDIVIDUAL AND GOD.

elects to be either the hermit or the free-lance instead of the member of the Body.

Yet, with all this full in view, I think it is seasonable to emphasize the other side of things. I spoke in passing of distortions, travesties, impossibilities, sometimes to be met with in the advocacy of Church life and work. It is so. Definitions or descriptions of the Church are often attempted which square neither with reason nor Scripture. In the nature of the case, in this world of the Fall, ideal and actual never coincide. So Augustine long ago was constrained to own, when Donatism pressed the matter on his mind. "Not only in eternity, but now," he says,* "hypocrites" (the unreal) "are not associated with Christ, however they may *seem to be* in His Church." Forgetting this, good men have tried to define the Church in terms which cannot but burst and yield when compared with the great Scriptural tests, negative and positve, of incorporation into the Lord. And so is invited a resistance which runs easily into an opposite and really individualistic extreme. For the thought has tended towards a spiritual tyranny, in which the Church becomes the autocrat of conscience, and even the temperate assertion of conscience against the autocracy is taken as a kind of treason. So, two centuries ago, the Roman community, ruled by the

* De Doctrina Christiana, iii. 32.

Jesuit school, strove only too successfully to crush the Jansenist protest, made by some of the noblest Christians France, or Europe, ever saw—Pascal among them; reluctant and distressed assertors of conscience against the corporate idea. That case represents—how many other cases of the past, and of today!

Great is the place and function of the Church! But that place is not between the soul and the Redeemer. It is in the stress it has laid upon that truth that the Protestant principle has done one of its noblest services to the world. I found many years ago a testimony to this in an unbiased quarter, in an essay by the late Mr. J. S. Mill, on the Positive Philosophy, printed in the *Westminster Review* of April, 1865. Mill examines Comte's estimate of types of Christianity, and takes him to task for his complete misreading of Protestantism, as if it were only negative, only destructive; a mistake made by a great many persons besides Comte, but only possible for them, as for him, by defect of knowledge. "Comte," says Mill, " misses one of the most important facts connected with Protestantism—its remarkable efficacy, as contrasted with Catholicism" (he means Romanism), "in cultivating the intelligence and the conscience of the individual believer. The feeling of a direct responsibility of the individual immediately to God is almost wholly a creation of Protestantism. Even when Protestants were nearly as persecuting as Catholics (quite as much so they never were), still they maintained that the true belief was not to be accepted from a priest, but to be sought and found by the believer; and that no one could answer to God for him; he must answer for himself." And Mill, standing himself outside all creeds as he then stood (but I have heard privately what gives me right to think he died in the faith of Christ), goes on to comment, as well he may, upon the power of this view of things to give stuff and fiber to character, personal and national, wherever it prevails.

Yes; let the sacred function of the Community be what it may, it must stand aside, after all, and leave the ground open, when the soul, the mysterious personality, the man, rises up and goes in to claim in Christ its access to the Father, awful, blissful and in secret. "As for me, nearness to God for me is good." For this, man was made in his creation, waking up from the inscrutable mystery of its process to the mighty fact that he was in the image of his Maker. For this he was made again out of the death and ruins of the Fall. Because of the Cross, and in the power of the Spirit, he is admitted, he is entitled, he is welcomed as with open arms to an intercourse with God, mediated to him by the Son of God alone, nothing between. Lift high the curtains of the Holiest, for he must enter; yea, they are already rent from the top to the bottom, that he may pass within them, and stand with unveiled face before the secret glory, and speak his whole heart out to the heart of the Eternal, μετὰ παρρησίας, "with the liberty of *saying anything*" to his Father. Let no Society, though divinely founded, no ordinance, though of Christ's own giving, yet needing mortal ministration, no sacred Class or Order, however apostolic in succession, pass in with him there. True, they can, and they should, help him thither, show him the avenue, point him to the door, reassure him of the rightness of his entrance. But he enters, himself alone, or rather, himself as one with the one eternal Priest who stands there in His own right, who has offered once for ever the sacrifice of peace, and now for ever is occupied with that other and resultant function of His solitary and sublime *sacerdotium*—to be man's open entrance in to God.

The whole record of Redemption is full of that entrance in. Such was the divine delight in it that, ages before the historic and, as it were, public opening of the door, there was already a wonderful anticipation. The saints of the Old Law are found

THE INDIVIDUAL AND GOD.

speaking their souls out to the Lord as the breath and habit of their lives—nothing between, absolutely nothing, but the fact of the promise and the covenant. True, their colloquies with God were of infinite significance to the community. Abraham under the Syrian stars, Moses on the desert cliff, Jeremiah in the courtyard in the beleaguered town, not only supplied examples of individual "access;" their conversations with heaven made links in the story of the redemption of the world. But, none the less, it was in itself individual intercourse, personal, direct; "nothing between." It was not the individual approaching God through the mediation of the community. A vast element in the phenomenon of Scripture is the precise converse; the voice of grace reaches the community through the mediation of the individual believer.

Think of the magnificent illustration of this in the Old Testament, in the Book of Psalms. No doubt the Psalms for the Jewish Church, as for the Church Catholic, bore a liturgical significance; they passed into common worship; they became the voice of the community to God. And obviously many of them are public and corporate in their form—the expression of the experiences of the chosen Race in its collective sins and disciplines and blessings. But set these aside, they leave a mass rich and wonderful of purely individual Psalms, in which rises just the call and cry of the Ego to the Eternal. "I have trusted in Thy mercy; my heart shall be glad in Thy salvation;" "I will fear no evil, for Thou art with me;" "My soul thirsteth for the living God;" "Thou hast known my soul in adversities;" "I love the Lord, because He hath heard my voice;" "Thy Word is a lamp unto my feet;" "Thou art my portion;" "As for me, I will behold Thy face in righteousness;" "As for me, nearness to God for me is good."

Whatever part in the ages of the Psalmists was played by the order and ritual of the Society, the man, for his soul's inmost needs, was left alone with God; the servant went in to his Master to talk with Him, and the door was shut.

To pass into the New Testament in order to study individual converse with God is to take the clue of a labyrinth endless in its depth and beauty. Of this the words and the works of the Redeemer alike are full. "I will; be thou clean;" "I will in no wise cast him out;" "I will manifest myself to him." The incidents of the Acts are perpetually individualistic: the Eunuch in his carriage, Cornelius in his chamber, Lydia by the river. Above all, we have Saul of Tarsus, the man chosen by the Spirit to contribute a third of its contents to the New Testa-

THE INDIVIDUAL AND GOD.

ment, and to develop all that is most comprehensive and collective in the message of our salvation, but led to do all this in modes of exposition where the widest, the vastest principles come to us alive and pulsating with the experiences of the man with God. "In me there dwelleth no good thing;" "I am crucified with Christ;" "Christ liveth in me;" "He gave Himself for me;" "I can do all things in Him;" "I know whom I have believed;" "He is able to keep my deposit against that day."

My brethren, this is a magnificent individualism, sanctifying, beautifying, vital. I hope I have guarded myself from seeming to forget the other side in the spiritual life. I have tried to label with as legible a censure as I could the falsehood of the individualism which means isolation to one's own will, isolation even to one's own soul. But this is another thing; yea, in its depth it is the antithesis to that. This is an isolation to God, in the immediate intercourse of the regenerate soul with Him, an intercourse whose very possibility is denied, as you know, by arbitrary and *a priori* speculation, but in vain; *E pur si muove* —it is an experienced fact. This is an isolation which sends the soul out again, filled and expanded by His presence, to contribute to the community, to live no longer for itself, to be at His service in others all the day, aye, and to see deeper into others, their struggles, their sorrows, and their sins, than it ever could do if it did not know itself in the light of intercourse with God. For that intercourse there is no substitute; it knows no second-best. Would we be "men in Christ" indeed? Then, "as for me, nearness to God for me is good."

More than ever in our late and troubled time, so intensely conscious in some of its aspects, so superficial in others, the Christian must guard and use his personal "access with confidence," through the Son, in the Spirit, to the Father.

He will find his exercise of it imperiled from many quarters. Sometimes, as we have remembered, a mental theory will try to shut the door brusquely in his face, with a doctrine of knowledge which is to prove, forsooth, that God cannot personally converse with the personality which He made in His own image. Sometimes an overwrought ecclesiasticism will not precisely bar the door, but load it with curtains, offering rather the assistance of a third party to carry the messages in and out. Far oftener the obstruction will come from that common disposition of our period, with its unrest, its fatigues, its materialistic ideals of good—the slack and indolent disposition to "get our religion done for us," in one way or another. But it matters little, by comparison, how the temptation meets us, under what mask the watchful enemy will try to impede our personal intercourse with the Everlasting Friend. It is vital, anyhow, that we should resist, and enter in.

"Nearness to God," face to face, is vital, if we would live the life which alone is real, ἡ ὄντως ζωή. "This is the life eternal, to *know*—to know the only true God, and Jesus Christ whom He hath sent." And that knowledge cannot possibly be got at second hand.

"Nearness to God" is vital, if we would be pure. Would we have, would we retain, cleanness—not of hands only, but of heart—inwardly and to the depth? It is the man who "hath the hope in Him that when He shall appear we shall be like Him, seeing Him as He is," who "purifieth himself even as He is pure."* And to see Him then we must have seen Him now, as personal faith alone sees "Him who is invisible." Intercourse with God is the victorious secret of heart-purity—intercourse direct, individual, alone. The outward and inward foes to purity are strong and subtle: woe to the man who undertakes them in his own name! But there is a power, which the weakest Christian can seek, and find, and wield, which is adequate for their absolute defeat: "they shall fall and perish *at Thy presence*."

"Nearness to God" is vital, if we would be un-

* 1 John iii. 2, 3.

wearied amidst a world indifferent, even when not positively corrupted, in the active strife for virtue. They tell us that there is a perceptible decline in England of strong enthusiasm for great moral causes. Is it so? Then contribute your own weight, at least, to the scale for virtue in her need against the mighty. And if you would do so in the right spirit, unhasting, unresting, patient, resolved, unembittered, absolutely convinced, be much in intercourse with God. They who would indeed move the world for righteousness need to have "the secret of His presence" about them "before the sons of men." And they must find that secret first—alone with Him.

"Nearness to God" is vital for the right entrance into all the energies and interests of a true life. You must live for your work, whatever work the eternal Master has chosen for you. You must live in it. You, Christian students, must live in your mental labor, and not play around its fringes. But you cannot live *on* it; your life-power is in your God, your Saviour; you must nourish it with Him, assimilating Him ever more in the healthy hunger of the soul. "He that eateth Me shall live because of Me." Yes, he shall live, he shall move, he shall indeed have power.

Sixty-two years ago, short of just three weeks,* in

* The Sermon was preached October 23, 1898.

THE INDIVIDUAL AND GOD.

his rooms at King's, while the bell of this Church was pealing for the sermon he was to have delivered, sinking down at last after fifty-four years of strenuous and vastly fruitful work in this place for Christ, died Charles Simeon, *clarum et venerabile nomen,* a glory to Eton, to Cambridge, to our English Christendom. If ever man labored, it was he; touching, you might have thought, the world around him with ceaseless activities in his every waking hour, so great was his record of tangible achievement. But no; day by day his earliest waking hours, won by brave self-discipline from sleep, were spent, all through his life from young manhood onwards, in solitary converse with God. His rooms were his oratory, and so was the roof above them, where he paced the leads alone in long intercourse with his Lord. Thence flowed out the life spiritually so powerful. His last surviving intimate, the honored William Carus, seven years ago, in the bedchamber at Bournemouth where shortly afterwards he passed radiant with love and happiness to the world of light, spoke once more to me of Simeon. And his thought was not of Simeon's energies, but of the source behind them. "That was a wonderful life," he said to me, "the life he lived up there, all alone with God."

In our day, in our measure, for our life, our strife, our toil, we also will seek and we shall find. "As for me, nearness to God for me is good."

VIII.

TWO CAMBRIDGE SAINTS: NICHOLAS RIDLEY, HENRY MARTYN

Preached in the University Church, Cambridge, October 16, 1898.

"Whose faith follow, considering the end of their conversation."—HEB. xiii. 7.

THIS sixteenth day of October, as it happens, is a date to be remembered in the Christian annals of Cambridge. It is the day on which two of our academic Mother's noblest sons, first one and then, after a long interval of time, the other, laid down their lives and slept in Christ.

On October 16, 1555, at Oxford, on a morning of torrent rain and fitful sunshine, at a stake set in Balliol ditch, in a fire lighted with difficulty and delay, and which did its fierce work only by degrees, died Nicholas Ridley, Bishop of London, late Bishop of Rochester, formerly Master of Pembroke in this University, "crying with a wonderful great voice: *In manus tuas, Domine, commendo spiritum meum,*" till the fire touched the bag of gunpowder, and the cry was stilled.

NICHOLAS RIDLEY, HENRY MARTYN.

On October 16, 1812, a young English clergyman, chaplain of the East India Company, broken with consumption and burnt with fever, alone of every European friend, trying to reach Constantinople for England by forced marches on horseback, expired in the town of Tocat, near the southern shores of the Black Sea. He was a Bachelor of our Divinity Faculty, a Fellow of St. John's; he had been placed Senior Wrangler, at the head of a brilliant list, eleven years before, in 1801. His name was Henry Martyn.

Thus a coincidence of the calendar brings together two lives and deaths, two names and characters, separated by great lengths of period and circumstance, but on the other hand closely akin to one another, in their relation to our beloved Cambridge, in richness of intellectual endowment, in the life of Christian faith and love, yea, the life hid with Christ in God, and in the call, each man after the conditions of his time, greatly to labor and greatly to suffer for their Lord.

It has occurred to me that a brief commemoration and consideration of these two lives and deaths may afford not unsuitable matter for our attention on this the first Sunday of full term in a new Cambridge year. Ridley and Martyn seem to me to be, each of them, a man singularly noble and suggestive as a type, a lesson, an animation. In particular, I seem to see in them inspiring examples of what I may call the University character, the character receptive of and developed by the highest influences of an English University. Widely differing in some respects, as two strong individualities of quite different periods would be likely to do, they had some great characteristics in common. They were eminently *men,* in the courage and in the gentleness which belong to the true man. Physically, each was remembered by his friends as strong and agile; mentally, they were gifted far above the common, and put their powers to indefatigable and lofty use. In habits of life they both appear to have shown that wholesome combination, the freedom of a perfect naturalness, of a kindly humor, of extended interests, along with a self-discipline which, rooted in the fear of God and nursed by an unswerving rule of secret devotion before Him, touched their whole conduct with its elastic but firm sway, preparing them to sacrifice even more than to achieve. Let it be added that, having well used the gifts and training of Cambridge, they both loved her to the end with a strong and beautiful affection. Martyn, in his letters from the remote East, perpetually recurs to her. Ridley, within a fortnight of the fire, writes his last letters of farewell to the scenes and persons of his life—one of the grandest flights, in my poor opinion, of all our older English prose, not excepting Milton's own; and deep and tender are the adieux he addresses there to his University and to his College.

As types of Englishmen, of Cambridge students, of believers in and servants of our Lord Jesus Christ, types differing yet deeply cognate, I think that Ridley and Martyn may well engage us for a little while. We will consider something of their "conversation," their life-course, and of its "end." I think we shall not deny that it is well with those who "follow," who imitate, "their faith."

Nicholas Ridley was son of a Northumbrian knight. I stood, last August, in what remains of the somewhat grim fortified house, Willimoteswick, or Willumswick, as the peasants call it, where first he saw the light, about 1503, on the hilly sides of Tynedale. Flodden was an event of his boyhood, and the associations of Border warfare lived in his memory to the end. In his Farewell he cheers his spirit for the last fiery conflict for what with all his soul he held for truth, by recalling how often he had seen his kinsfolk and neighbors stand for their hearths and homes, to the death, if need be, against the raiders of the North.

From school he passed to Pembroke here, and in 1522 his name appears in our ancient registers fourth among the Wranglers, indicating a successful study of the whole curriculum of his time. He was chosen Fellow, and at length Master, of his College, and took for some years an active part in the life and business of the University. On the accession of Edward he was called to the see of Rochester, as a man eminent for learning and godliness, and an avowed friend of the Reformation. From Rochester, three years later, he passed to London. Another short three years, and the advent of Mary and the restoration of the Papacy consigned him to prison in the Tower. Thence he was transferred to custody, and to the most unjust of trials, at Oxford. Eighteen months later, when, after a certain pause and intermission, the burnings began again, he was called with his elder colleague, Latimer, to die. At supper overnight he bade his friends to his marriage. He slept the night quietly out, and then the two heroic friends passed, if I may borrow the language of John James Blunt and of Julius Hare, "in their fiery chariot to heaven."

It would of course be altogether out of place and occasion to attempt to exhibit Ridley's life and work before you in any detail. It must be enough to recall a few outstanding facts. He was the diligent administrator of his College, and also, in his vacations, the laborious and studious parish priest of Herne, in Kent. As Bishop he appears to have won the respect even of theological and political opponents by his incessant labor as preacher and chief pastor, and by the beautiful and cheerful saintliness of his domestic life. It was a life single to the last, but eminently kindly and social, and full of winning charities. At Fulham he showed filial honor to the aged mother of his deprived predecessor, Bonner, setting her always, in whatever presence, in the best place at his table.

Altogether we seem to see in Nicholas Ridley a high example of the English gentleman and the true son of the English Church, as she moved forward into purer light at the Reformation. He was the man who, in his Pembroke days, was remembered for his love of archery, and of fives, and of chess, as well as for his tranquil piety and his large reading, as reading began to be understood in the period of Erasmus. He was the delightful converser at his episcopal table, the Christian father of his servants, the ardent friend of his friends in God, the practical and far-seeing advocate of the destitute poor. He was the dispassionate student of the great controversy of his time, and arrived, amidst stormy surroundings, in a serene conviction and without heat or hurry, at conclusions about the Papacy and about the sacred Eucharist which made an epoch—I presume to say, a great and most salutary epoch—in English theology. He was the courageous defender of the rights and property of Church and School against the greed of an unscrupulous Court, the unworthy circle around the high-souled and blameless Edward. In 1548, Clare Hall, now Clare College, would have been swept away for sordid purposes but for the resolute stand of Ridley against the Protector, Somerset. In things divine he was the reverent lover of the past as to all which was really primeval in it, and pure, and of good report; the indignant rebuker of the pseudo-protestant spirit which could make jests over eucharistic error. Yet he did not spare the associations of a lifetime when he conceived it his duty to advocate change in the cause of Christ and of His truth. No man that I have read of seems to me more finely to embody the ideal of the Anglican Reform, the character kindred to the spirit of the book of Common Prayer, with all its piety towards the past, and all its yet deeper piety towards spiritual truth and the open Scriptures, educating the soul and mind in a worship stately in its grave simplicity, and irradiated all over and all through with the light of a reason large and open, and with the glory of a free approach to God in Christ, for the whole Church equally and together, in spirit and in truth.

Such, faintly outlined, was Nicholas Ridley, as he was known. But the true life of the true man has its pulse, of course, far behind the scenes. And Ridley, alike in his prosperity and in his hours of outward ruin, lived the hidden life with God, conversing with Him over His sacred Word. In his Farewell, he lifts the veil from those secrets for a moment, when he bids adieu to his well-loved Pembroke: "In thy orchard (the walls, butts and trees, if they could speak, would bear me witness) I learned without book almost all Paul's Epistles, yea, and I ween all the canonical Epistles, save only the Apocalypse. Of which study, though in time a great part did depart from me, yet the sweet smell thereof I trust I shall carry with me into heaven."

Ridley's Walk is still shown in the grounds of Pembroke. And the memory of our other academic saint of to-day links itself also with a garden, a grove green and fair in all its bowery colonnades, the wilderness of St John's. Never do I pass the borders of that pleasant place but the mind seems almost to see, pacing its paths, rapt in thought and prayer, young Henry Martyn. It was his chosen resort for privacy, during the four years of his residence as a Fellow in his College. On the eve of his departure for the East he bade it farewell, on Saturday, April 6, 1805: "I passed most of the morning in the Fellows' garden. It was the last time I visited this favorite retreat, where I have often enjoyed the presence of God."

Henry Martyn was born at Truro, in 1781, son of a father who had been a working superintendent in the mines of Gwenap, and had raised himself to competence. He entered St. John's College in 1797. According to his own sorrowing admission, he came up careless of religion, and living altogether without prayer. His spirits were high and his temper vehement, and to please and to distinguish himself was his main purpose. Certainly he was well equipped for distinction. He arrived totally ignorant of the very elements of mathematics, yet he was head of his Tripos and first Smith's Prizeman within three years and a half; and this although his friends, as they afterwards recalled what he had been, were used to say that he was much more deeply interested in philology and in literature than in number and figure. A little later he took the prize for the Latin Essay over competitors of classical distinction.

But by this time he was a prayerless man no longer. In his second year, his father's death cast a shadow over earth's brightness for him, and the teaching and friendship of Charles Simeon, strongest and tenderest of Christian guides and helpers, was used to lead him to the feet of his Redeemer. Faith, as it ought to do, only quickened and elevated his intellectual life; he has left it on record that nature and letters both seemed to present to him new depths and beauties when he came to know the Lord. But with that knowledge came also, of course, the desire wholly to do His will; and His will, indicated in many ways, led him, within a few years, with Simeon's energetic and prescient encouragement, to devote himself to India—India, then remote from England as no inhabited region of the earth is remote today. He went out in 1805 as a Company's Chaplain, at a time when missionaries, as such, to the indescribable reproach of the then policy of the Directors, were interdicted within the British pale. But a chaplain had considerable freedom for occasional intercourse with the natives, and Martyn used the opportunity. He gave his whole mental power to Sanscrit, Hindoostanee, Arabic, and Persian. He preached whenever and wherever he could to native audiences; he did wonders of achievement as a translator within his seven short years of Indian life, and he powerfully impressed the most cultivated and skeptical Europeans by his union of literary faculty and acquirement with abundant cheerfulness, with attentive and faultless courtesy, and with the purest and most courageous godliness in daily life.

On furlough in Persia, where he traveled to perfect his Persian, he engaged often in discussion with the Mahometan and mystic sages, and earned now their threats and revilings as he confessed the Godhead of his Lord, and now their reverence as for the holiest and most learned of the Franks. Sick at last with the advances of mortal weakness, and with the sorrows of a pure human love disappointed (for the chosen of his heart was never free to join him in India), he set out on leave for England, and died upon the vast journey overland. At Tocat his dust now reposes; in the garden of the American Mission stands (or stood a while ago; we trust that the wave of outrage of these latter days has spared it) an obelisk over Martyn's grave, recording in four languages who he was and why he was buried there.

No English friend was with him at or near the end; but that Presence which never fails the faithful was not only about him, but felt and known to be about him, true to the promise of our King to those that love Him and do His will: "He that hath My commandments and keepeth them, he it is that loveth Me; and he that loveth Me shall be loved of My Father, and I will love him, and will manifest Myself to him."* Martyn's journal was carried on by his Tartar courier to Constantinople, and so reached England. Its latest entry, written at an unnamed place on the Persian border, is dated October 6, 1812, ten days before the end: "No horses being to be had, I had an unexpected repose. I sat in the orchard" (another orchard than that of Ridley's Pembroke), "and thought with sweet comfort and peace of my God, in solitude my company, my Friend and Comforter. Oh, when shall time give place to eternity? When shall appear that new heaven and new earth wherein dwelleth righteousness? There, there shall in no wise enter anything that defileth; none of those corruptions which add still more to the miseries of mortality shall be seen or heard of any more."

So he touched the brink of that mysterious Jordan which awaits our feet also, and so he passed over, finding without a doubt that great word true, "If a man keep My saying, he shall never see death."† He was but thirty-one years old, and he was never permitted to receive one genuine convert as the fruit of his personal Indian ministry; but for eighty-six years now his memory, his example, his pure flame

* John xiv. 21. † John viii. 51.

of "zeal and love, recorded eminent," has borne the fruit of a host of consecrations to the like labor, in the name of the same redeeming Lord.

I have attempted thus to place before you some slight memorials of these two saints and servants of God, men of our race and land and Church, men of our Mother Cambridge, each reflecting indeed a peculiar honor on his illustrious College here; but all such honors are our common property besides.

It is, of course, with serious purpose that I have spoken thus of Ridley and of Martyn. True, it is a personal delight to contemplate such characters and faces with a regard which for a while terminates in them; "it is good to look upon a man," above all, upon a man of God. But it can never possibly be well to let our sight of the saints really terminate in them. We can see them rightly only when they are asked to answer our gaze with their messages, and, above all, to point us upward to look upon their King.

As we prepare to close, then, what, in some great particulars, is the message of these two lives to us?

It comes partly through their differences. Not to speak of personal characteristics, Ridley and Martyn were called by their Disposer to walks and works widely differing. To the one was allotted the magnificent but formidable period of the Renaissance and the Reformation; to the other, a time in which, splendid as many of its features were, English culture had scarcely yet felt the full modern impulse, and when English religion was only struggling back with difficulty and by degrees into spiritual power after a long abeyance. To the one was assigned a public life and labor, extended over many years, a formative hand at a great crisis of the Church, a confession before unjust judges, and a death of shame and agony. The other was called to a work comparatively silent and private in its conditions, under alien skies, an experiment often rather than an achievement, to sickness, solitude, and an early grave.

Such were some of their differences. They speak to us the old message that "God fulfills Himself in many ways" in His saints—in divers manners as well as at sundry times; and they remind us that for every life here, for every mind, for every will, for every hand, so it be given over to the hand of God, there lies ready the chosen and adjusted faith and task, no two quite alike, "to every man *his* work."

But the differences all run up, in Ridley and in Martyn, into great features of likeness, of identity.

Their lives were both of a piece, for one thing, in their energetic and conscientious use of the gifts of God, as well as of His grace, that gift which we must rank apart. The academic stories of the two are indeed akin. The Fourth Wrangler of 1522 and the Senior Wrangler of 1801 were both men who knew the sacredness of the gift of mind, and in the scene of study made it their first duty to be students, reaping from this a harvest of power for their work to come. Their lives, again, were of a piece as time called them on to action, in respect of the recognition of the special work, allotted to their periods, the purpose and power to "serve their own generation in the will of God." Nobly forgetful of ease and self-protection, and never dreaming of the poor, the pitiable, question, whether their convictions were popular and in the fashion, they addressed themselves, the one to his part in the great crisis of the national Church, the other to the dawning hope of the evangelization of the world, as to the call of their Master then and there for them.

But the deepest of all their likenesses, the thing, rather, in which they were one—I beseech my brethren, and you, my younger brethren, especially, to recollect and weigh it—was their personal relation to Jesus Christ our Lord. In this, Ridley and Martyn meet indeed and, as it were, are merged together. Historically, their theology of His Person, and also of His saving Work, was the same and one. In spiritual experience, they knew, and they lived by, the same certainties about Him. The mighty truths recovered publicly for the Church at the Reformation, and called into fresh and wonderful effect in the memorable Revival of the eighteenth century, the truth of Justification by Faith, that is, of peace with God in a trusted Christ, and the truth of the living Work of the Holy Spirit, free and personal, glorifying Christ in the heart—these truths, could we have put the question to them, would have been affirmed with equal joy by the martyr of Oxford and the confessor of Tocat.

They were what they were because of Him. Christ in His merit for them, Christ in His life in them, this was the last analysis of their "conversation" and of its "end."

To them, even as it must be to the latest of all human generations, to "whosoever will come after Him," He was not something only, nor much only, but all—all for the burthened conscience, all for the wandering and the fainting will, and for the mortal mystery at last. With Him, as with their living Law and Peace and Hope and Power, they lived conversing. And so they caught His likeness on their faces, till in each of them we see something of

Him. (And, oh, what dream of other ambitions can ever soar so high at its utmost flight as the hope that through the disciple may be somehow seen some scintilla of the MASTER'S brightness?) As Isaac Taylor says, in a pregnant essay in his *Saturday Evening:* "So far as Christians truly exhibit the characteristics of their Lord, in spirit and conduct, a vivid emotion is enkindled in other Christian bosoms, as if the bright Original of all perfection stood dimly revealed. The conclusion comes upon the mind that this family resemblance springs from a common center, and that there exists, as its archetype, an invisible Personage, of whose glory all are in a measure partaking."

So it was then, so it is now; for "Jesus Christ is the same, yesterday, and today, and unto the ages too."

IX

THE SIGHT OF SELF AND THE SIGHT OF CHRIST

Preached in the University Church, Oxford

"When I saw Him, I fell at His feet as dead. And He laid His right hand upon me, saying unto me, Fear not; I am the First and the Last: I am He that liveth, and was dead; and, behold, I am alive for evermore, Amen; and have the keys of hell and of death."—Rev. i, 17, 18.

I READ these words with a very simple purpose. They lie surrounded with mystery for their context, and in their own terms they all "go off into mystery." But I approach them for no elaborate inquiry; I accept them as they stand. Here, in the faith of the Church of Christ, verified by the heavenly Spirit to the believing soul, is a true record of a true experience, when on that far-off Lord's Day, upon the rock of Patmos, John of Galilee, venerable, saintly, full of the Holy Ghost and of the powers of the world to come, fell down as if dead at the feet of his manifested Master. Then and there was he touched by that Master's hand, while there came upon his soul, not from within him but from without, his Master's utterance. What spoke to him was no mere issue of the action of his mind. It was Christ's heart in Christ's words. It was He, putting Himself in contact with the disciple; it was He, telling him that he need not fear, and that the reason not to fear lay altogether and forever in Him who touched him.

It is tempting to try to collect in the mind the astonishing imagery of the vision; as if we could figure to ourselves the seer in his prostration, and above him the Human Face which shone like the sun, and the moving lips whose words were like the voices of the sea. But such attempts at a misnamed realization can do us little good. It is better to fall back at once upon the inmost essence of the scene, and so to realize it indeed. Behold the *spiritual* phenomenon. Consider this prostration of the mortal disciple—yes, though he is also the chosen friend of the Incarnate God. See him collapsed before his Lord thus manifested to his spirit, till he rises and revives only by the deed and word of that Lord Himself. With this direct and simple purpose I place this Scripture before you, asking you to suffer me in a few remembrances and appeals over two large truths embodied in the Epiphany, the Theophany, of Patmos. Standing within its solemn glory, let us first consider how man sees himself in the act of seeing the Son of God; then, how he is told not to fear, in the Name, and only in the Name, of Him whom he has seen.

May He, merciful and gracious, not leave us alone with the subject of Himself. Without Him, our essays of thought upon Him are sure to be futile and beside the mark. But let Him be with us and we shall not think in vain of what He is.

i. Here first, then, we have before us man seeing himself, in the act of seeing the King, the Lord God, the Lamb of God, the Son of the Father. He sees Him, and is overwhelmed in seeing.

This, on the threshold, is a profound paradox. Thanks be to God, Christians have learned to combine habitually with the thought of the sight of Christ ideas of great peace and joy. "I said, Behold Me;" "Look unto Me, and be ye saved." "He that seeth the Son," he that gazeth upon the Son—ὁ θεωρῶν τὸν Υἱόν.— "and believeth on Him, hath eternal life." "Now lettest Thou Thy servant depart in peace, for mine eyes have seen Thy salvation, the Lord's Christ." And that association of thoughts is divinely just. To look thither, to contemplate the Only Begotten, to behold the Lamb of God, to do that effortless work, to learn the blissful quietism of that look of faith, is life indeed. Who that has had his tired and bewildered eyes at length lifted to that open vision, he knows not how, can ever cease to rest and to be glad in the light of it, knowing with an insight which passes beyond analysis that in his manifested Lord is really present for him, now and always, a repose, a strength, a light, a gladness which is ultimate, and satisfies? But then, this is only so because of the revelation of grace seen along with the revelation of glory. It is because of the mercifully revealed relation between the majesty of Christ and the salvation of the beholder of it. Remove the thought of that relation; place together, in the way, not of contact but of contrast, the seer and the Object of his sight, and it is otherwise then. Then, if the sinner's insight into Christ is at all spiritually true, he falls at His feet as dead. "In His light we see light"; but we see darkness too; we see self, we see the foulness and the guilt of sin, and the awful rightfulness which utters over it the sentence of a final exile into the outer night.

So it is all through the Scriptures. Primal man, fallen out of concord with the will of God, hides himself in the deep bower from that approaching Voice of awful and eternal sweetness.* Abraham stands at Mamre talking with his Divine Friend; and on a sudden he knows through his inmost being

* Gen. iii. 8.

AND THE SIGHT OF CHRIST. 151

that he is dust and ashes.* Young Isaiah, in his temple-trance,† sees 'the King, the Lord of Hosts'; none other (if St. John‡ may be our expositor here) than the Christ of God; and he cries out that he is undone. Job is pronounced perfect by God Himself in the opening scene; but he gets at the end an insight into the Creatorship of the Eternal, which instantly lifts him (it is even so that the fully awakened spirit reasons) to an insight into His holiness, and then he clasps his hand to his mouth, and abhors himself, and repents.§ Peter in the Galilean fishing-boat feels Heaven near him in his Master— and he implores Him to go away.‖ Saul falls helpless and confounded when, in one tremendous moment, he sees the glorified Jesus without having yet believed on Him. And here, last of all, is John, the intimate, the chosen friend, the dear disciple, nearest of the near in that sweet intercourse of old; he too sees in a terrible sunlight what Christ is—in contrast with a saint; and he falls at His feet as dead.

Here is indeed conviction of sin. It is not only conviction of creaturehood, of frailty, of mortality; it is conviction of sin. No one can ponder the parallel scenes (for example, the scene where Isaiah

* Gen. xviii. 27. † Isairh vi. 5. ‡ John xii. 41.
§ Job i. 8, xlii. 5, 6. ‖ Luke v. 8.

sees God, and cries aloud that he is a lost man), and can doubt that John also, in this moment of vision, felt in the very basis of his being that awful difference between fallen man and God which is sin; that ὑστέρημα, — that "falling short of His glory,"* which man may totally ignore in his easy hour, or at the most may attenuate and extenuate, but which in the hour of spiritual vision he sees as a gulf immeasurable, impassable, except by the mercy of the Holy One.

To see God, aye to see God in Christ, in a light which shows His holiness, but which is not yet transmitted through the revelation of redeeming love, is an awful thing. "At this also the heart trembleth, and is moved out of its place." "No man shall see My face and live."

Yet, my brethren, suffer me humbly to affirm that, awful as that sight is, it is divinely salutary. Deep in the heart of all genuine human holiness lies conviction of sin, the spiritual sense of sin, the having been brought in truth and fact to something of Job's abhorrence and John's prostration. I do not mean a morbid and restless introspection. What I mean is not so much inlook as outlook. It is not to dwell with a perilous minuteness upon the pathology of particular sins; this may be only the distorted

* Rom. iii. 23.

counterfeit of a true self-examination. I mean something at once deeper and higher: a waking up of conscience to the awfulness of sin as sin; to the spiritual fact that sin is the thing eternally abominable to the living God; to the sight of it in the light of His pure law, till sin, in the stern tautology of the Apostle,* becomes to us "exceedingly sinful," because it is discord with the Will of God.

Such conviction has never been common. Is it too much to say that in our own time it is even more than usually scarce, and strange, and out of the religious fashion? Yet it affects the very life of the soul, and so of the Church. Has any great misbelief ever arisen in Christendom, and there has not lain at its roots an enfeebled sense of sin? It has been said, and I for one hold it for truth, that the proof and certainty of the Faith is fully seen only through the awakened conscience. Then let us ask, and seek, and knock for conviction of sin. For the sake of the depth and firmness of our faith in Christ, and of our peace in submission to His will, and of our serviceableness for His work, let us dare to welcome the conviction, deep and sacred, of the sinfulness of sin.

For this end, if only for this, let us set ourselves anew to consider "the Inhabitant of Eternity, whose

* Rom. vii. 13.

name is Holy."* Let us often visit the ground (not too much frequented now) where man puts his shoes off his feet before God. Let us receive into our religion the spirit of holy fear, that untormenting but worshiping fear which apprehends the purity of the King of Saints, which wonders at His mercy as well as takes it; which exclaims with Micah,† "Who is a God like unto Thee, that pardoneth iniquity?" while yet we see, with a faith only the clearer for that holy wonder, that He stands engaged (so that same Scripture tells us) "to subdue our iniquities and to cast all our sins into the sea."

Such worshiping insights do not come to spiritual indolence. They want wakeful care, and guarded hours, that men may be alone before their Lord. They want a humble submission to the heavenly Word, with a willingness that light should fall through it direct upon our darkness. But we shall be well recompensed for the watching and the submission. The sight of the Holy One is the most abasing of all things, but it is the secret of all joy. It is well to reach that joy by learning first what it is to have *nothing to say for ourselves*—that vital factor in true repentance; and we learn this in the sight of Christ's glory. Let us covet such sights of Him as shall let us fall at His feet *with nothing*

*Isa. lvii. 15.   † Mic. vii. 18, 19.

at all to say. It is good to be there, and to be so. To be so there is to be beneath the touch of His hand, within the sound of His voice, as He says to us, what only He has the right to say, "Fear not."

ii. With that word we are brought to the second limb of the text. We come to find the man, thus broken down by the sight of the Holy One, now raised and reassured and greatly blest in the name of Him whom he has seen. "He woundeth, and His hands make whole."

Here, again, in these last pages of the Bible, we have a spiritual phenomenon traceable through the whole Volume. Always, where man finds himself confounded before God, it is from God Himself and from no alien region that the wonderful reassurance comes. When Isaiah says, "I am undone," the Seraph from above the throne brings him the fiery sacrament* of pardon and of power. Job abhors himself because his eye sees the Lord, and the Lord personally accepts him, with abundant welcomes. Peter shrinks in the boat away from his Master, and his Master says, "Be not afraid." And here at Patmos it is the same: "He laid His right hand upon me, saying unto me, Do not fear; I am the First and the Last, and the Living One; and I became dead; and behold living am I to the endless

* Isa. vi. 6.

ages, Amen; and I have the keys of Hades and of death." This is revival and reassurance to purpose; a strong consolation, for its material and texture is altogether Jesus Christ. Not a word is said of any reason not to fear inherent in the disciple; not a syllable comes, in that transcendent moment, about the endeared and wonderful past of Galilee and of Judea, those incidents of the most sacred of all friendships, in the cottage, in the field, on the shore, on the waters, on the hills. For the season, it is as if earth were not, and John were isolated and solitary in eternity, simply a sinner, cast down before the glory of the Son of God. And the reason for the "Do not fear" does not attach itself to John at all. It is not, "It is thou." It is altogether, "It is I."

"It *sets* Him well to commend Himself"; so said an aged disciple, in a northern cottage, about her Lord and Saviour. "It sets Him, it becomes Him well to commend Himself." Certainly it is characteristic of His thought and utterance to do so. Meek and lowly of heart, He is yet true to Himself, and, being what He is, He must say the thing that is. As in the days of His flesh, so here in these of His glory, our Lord Jesus Christ is His own gospel. He puts Himself into contact with the man at His feet, laying upon him the hand which by its touch is to signify and seal at once His claim, His blessing, and that immediate union which His grace sets up between Himself and His redeemed. And then He tells him not to fear. And then, in order to this, He recites the roll of His own majesty and mercy. "I am the First and the Last, and the Living One"— ὁ Ζῶν. He avows Himself originally and indefectibly Eternal; He is, He lives, from the Alpha that never began to the Omega that cannot end. He is no unknowable Infinity. But He is Infinite, and to be so known. In His timeless and necessary Oneness with the Father, it is His not to become but to be, with a Being full of the Fount of life. "And I became dead"— καὶ ἐγενόμην νεκρός a mysterious paradox, in which a most wonderful event is inserted, incorporated, into that eternity of being. In this short phrase He intimates the whole mystery of the Incarnation; but He presents just that aspect of it— short phrase He intimates the whole mystery of the Incarnation; but He presents just that aspect of it— mark it well—which sinful man, prone at His feet, most needs. He does not articulate the thought now of His blessed Birth, nor of His life, His speech, His labor, His example; there is nothing said here of Bethlehem, or of the years of Nazareth, or of the fair borders of the Lake with the furrowed fields, and the floating fishing-craft, and the listening multitudes upon the flowery slopes. It is all the Cross; it is only and altogether the precious Death and Burial. "I became dead." We read that sentence in the light of the long Apocalypse, and what do we see within it? The shame and glory of the Crucifixion, the atoning and redeeming Blood, the sacrifice of the Lamb, the Lamb not of innocence only but of the altar—"as it had been slain."

Yes, the Lord's Death, in its peculiar, its unique significance, appears always in these last pages of Scripture as the central, concentrating Fact, given for the wonder and worship of the heavenly elders and the innumerable redeemed in the upper glory. "Thou wast slain, and hast made purchase by Thy blood out of every kindred"; "Worthy is the Lamb that hath been slain." And here first with His own hand He strikes the theme of the mighty fugue— "I became dead," naming explicitly His Death alone out of all the history of His Humanity. Only, and of course, He gives it not as isolated; He glorifies it at once with His Resurrection. Without that, the Death would be to us as nothing. Without the Resurrection the Cross would speak to us no peace. In the field of history, without the Resurrection, the Cross would long since have faded into obscure and conflicting shadows; it would seem now at best one more pathetic ruin of illusory beliefs, soon dropped out of the speech and at last out of the heart of the weak votaries of a defeated and mistaken leader. But "Behold, living am I, for the endless ages, and I have the keys of Hades and of death." So the Prince of the Cross stands over His prostrate servant, to touch him, and to tell him not to fear. It is not the slain One merely, but the slain One risen, Master of Life, Abolisher of Death, He who has passed victorious through the deep Unseen and carried out its keys with Him, to hold for ever. The Risen Christ! Hear His Voice, feel His hand! It is "Christ which is our Life," for all this moment's necessities of the soul, the man. And it is Christ the imperial Ruler of the world of spirits, that world so awful to human apprehension out of Him, but in Him—for the man in Him—safe, hallowed, happy. The hand that rests so gently on the contrite servant is the hand which grasps the keys of death. All things there, as well as here, belong to those who belong to Him. Are you Christ's? Then "all things are yours"; not only "Paul, and Apollos, and Cephas," but also "life," and also, quite as truly, "death." *

So in the great vision the Lord glorifies Himself. "It sets Him well." He has to transfigure the trance of fear into the rest of faith, and He goes the nearest

* 1 Cor. iii. 22, 23.

way to do it. "I am He"; "It is I"; "Fear not."
John is lifted, in a single action, out of himself, to
find instant and absolute peace in Christ—Christ
eternal, sacrificed, risen, Lord of both worlds, and
in living contact with His servant.

What was so then is so to-day. In all other
things "the same, yesterday, and today, and for
ever," our Lord Jesus Christ is in nothing more
magnificently the same than in this—that He,
for the forgiveness, the acceptance, the peace,
the purification, the empowering of the sinful soul
of man, is, not something, not many things, not
the great things, but *all*. John's glorious brother
Paul, whose conversion still sheds on the Church
its great ray of witness to the Lord's eternal
power to subdue, to justify, to glorify—what says
Paul* of that all-sufficiency? "Of God are ye,
in Christ Jesus, who of God is made unto us
wisdom, even righteousness, and sanctification, and
redemption." All is there. The vast range of our
need is met by the circle, the faultless sphere, of
His supply. Righteousness, to justify the ungodly;
Sanctification, to separate us from sin to the living
fulness of a life in God; Redemption, body and

* 1 Cor. i. 30.

soul, into the final glory; such is Christ. He does not only give this. He is this. Christ is all.

Great and multifold is "the truth as it is in Him." The central facts of grace themselves, to think of them only, have aspects innumerable. But they all stand in relation to the sublime simplicity of the inmost heart of the Christian Gospel; out of that relation they cease to be. That Heart of the system is our personal Lord Jesus Christ; Christ all things *for* the Christian, Christ all things *in* him.

What gives to *faith,* man's faith, its peculiar and supreme position in the scheme of grace, from our side? Why does St. Paul, but quite equally St. John, and, above all, their Master, so emphasize and accentuate the call for faith? It is not because of the merit, because of the virtuousness, because of the beauty, of faith. Faith's essence is to look out of and ignore itself, to forget itself, to be forgotten, to be in a sense as if it were not. *Virtus fidei est virtus objecti.* Faith's power lies in what it touches, in the boundless adequacy and excellency of its divine Correlative, its glorious Object. It lies in the Virtue of Him to whom we bring nothing but our unutterable need, that we may take from Him His all. It lies in the fact that it is a void made for Jesus Christ; it is a hand held empty for that golden gift, Himself.

"God doth justify the believing man," writes Richard Hooker, a name bright and venerable in Oxford if anywhere, "not for the worthiness of his faith, but for the worthiness of Him which is believed."*

Would we then believe indeed unto the life eternal? Would we, in these days of uncertainties and unrest, gravitate to our center, and be at peace? Then let us not too much scrutinize and analyze our believing; let us rather acquaint ourselves with Jesus Christ. Christ, seen in His fulness, is the all-powerful magnet of faith. Get but a real view of Him, even through the scarcely rifted clouds, and we shall not question whether we can do so great a thing as to believe; we shall of course believe (may I dare to put it so?) in so great and so immeasurably good an Object. The traveler over the ocean, asked to embark upon a raft, ἐπὶ σχεδίας κινδυνεύειν, may reasonably falter. Invited to step upon the giant structure of the steamship, to enter some *Lucania* or *Campania,* he trusts wholly, so far as human warrants of safety can possibly go; but he forgets his reliance, in the vast reason for it, and he addresses himself to the business of his voyage.

But let our look upon that Object be the look of

* *Discourse of Justification,* ch. 33.

those who rely upon it, wholly indeed, but not *lightly*. Let it be the look of the contrite, who have fallen at His feet, and there felt His hand, and there heard His voice, deep as many waters, sweet as the love of God: "Fear not; for it is I, Fear not, because of Me. I am the First and the Last; I live; I died; I am alive for ever; I hold the keys."

X
"LOVEST THOU ME?"

Preached in the Chapel Royal, St. James's Palace

"Jesus saith to Simon Peter, Lovest thou Me?"—JOHN xxi. 15-17.

WHO that takes any delight in the Bible at all does not take delight in the twenty-first chapter of St. John? Who has not felt the benignant spell of that narrative, in its indescribable simplicity and depth, its gracious beauty and its soul-penetrating power? Willingly we follow the last Apostle as he recounts to us, in his uttermost age, with the photographic precision of an old man's recollection of his prime, that wonderful memory. He leads us as if into the very landscape of the Syrian lake. We embark with him in the boat, as if we heard the rattle of the oars, and the lap of the ripples on the sides. We "ply the watery task" with him and his comrades, as if we saw the vernal stars reflected under our eyes in the dusky mirror of the deep. Their weariness and disappointment, as the night wanes and they have taken nothing, are as if our own. And then comes up the morning over the dark hills of Moab, and there stands a Figure on

"LOVEST THOU ME?"

the solitary beach, and there are callings to and fro between beach and boat; and the nets are full and heavy on a sudden, and the disciple plunges into the water, to swim and wade to his Master's feet. The whole group soon gathers round the fire of coals; the fast is broken; and then there is a colloquy about love and labor and martyrdom and following. We have seen it, heard it, shared it all.

It was my happiness a few years ago to set eyes upon the Lake of Galilee, gazing with strange emotions upon the waters and the mountain-shores from the garden of the Scottish Mission Hospital (scene of a noble work for God) at Tiberias, and afterwards from a boat, built probably on lines unaltered for two thousand years, and worked by fishermen, clad probably in the very fashion of the Apostles. Wonderful was the charm of the thought that this was indeed the scene of the Gospels; the eyes of the Son of Man knew just those outlines of cliff, and field, and shore, and that snowy dome of Hermon looking on from the northern horizon. His feet trod this shell-wrought strand, aye, and the waves too into which those smooth waters can be tossed so soon. Somewhere yonder, on the further side (for surely it was on that more solitary margin), this last scene of St. John's narrative was enacted; *there* was kindled the ruddy fire, *there* the water flashed into silver as Simon Peter wrestled his way through. Along that shore, whose line lies so distinct between lake and hills, he followed the steps of Jesus, and turned to see John following too.

It was a moving thing to look thus with waking eyes on the region as it is. Yet, such is the power, the artless magic, of the narrative of the Apostle, that I know not whether the actual gain to realization was very great. The Gospel had created so visible a landscape that the eyes had less to add to the picture than I had hoped.

Yes, we may all in thought sit together by that fair water, abundantly assured that St. John's picture is as truthful as it is living, alike in scenery and in action. We may draw nearer to the spot in thought than I could draw by sight on that bright afternoon of my visit; for our mental steps may tread, as my feet could not do, that further strand, and we may pause within sight and hearing of the very dialogue. Look then, and listen. Jesus, in our hearing, is asking Simon, the son of Jonas, *"Lovest thou Me?"*

That we may better apprehend the depth and wonder of that question, and its significance for ourselves, let us stand by a little while and contemplate the Inquirer and the Answerer, and their relation to each other. It is Jesus Christ asking; it is Simon, son of Jonas, who is to reply.

"LOVEST THOU ME?"

Ecce Homo!—"Behold this Man," who requests the assurance of the other's personal affection! As to guise and garb (we may certainly take that for granted). He sits there, as much as ever, "in fashion as a man." Yes, the group gathered round the glowing embers by the lake-side is eight—seven disciples, bodily present, real men; one Master, bodily present, real man. He wears the dress of His country; He speaks with its accent; the morning sun throws His shadow upon the grass and the stones. Yes; but also, He is the Son of God, the Bearer of the sin of the world, the Savior of the world, the Conqueror—the recent Conqueror—of the grave. He has died the most mysterious of deaths, because man has sinned, and in order that man may be redeemed and saved. He now is alive for evermore, in the power of an endless and indissoluble life. Yet a little while and He will quit the visible. He will ascend, to enter the Unseen and to take His place on nothing less than the universal Throne. He will have a great place—"at the right hand of the Majesty on high, angels and authorities and powers being made subject unto Him."

Nor is He unconscious of His ineffable dignities. All through this scene by the lake St. John sets the Lord before us as speaking and acting with an autocratic majesty only the more impressive because of its absolute calm and ease. He claims to be the center and repose of the whole devotion of His disciples. He asserts, if the word *assert* can be used without obscuring His omnipotent quiet, the most absolute possible lordship over them, irresponsible and ultimate: "If I will that he tarry till I come, what is that to thee?" They, these Apostles, are His mere property. And the souls for which they are to labor equally belong to Him—"My lambs," "My sheep."

Such is the one Party in the scene—our Lord Jesus Christ, God and Man, in the serenity and loftiness of His resurrection life; Master and Commander, as He has just shown Himself to be, alike of nature and of man; "Head over all things" to creation, to the Church, and to the soul. From Him those simplest imaginable human syllables come upon the morning air, *Do you love me?*

Consider the other party in his turn. To us, indeed, the man and the name are great and venerable, as we think what St. Peter was in the sum of his life, and what his work means for the Church forever, and as we remember his present glorified rest and joy above. But it is no irreverence to recall the other side, as it showed itself there and then. Who is this man who receives that question, and prepares to answer? He is just a provincial, a peasant, born and bred in a corner, trained to common toil; a young man, we may assume, for surely the Apostles all belonged to their Master's generation—a young man, Galilean to the core, uncultured, plebeian, and, in point of character, "not so much strong as strongly marked";* impulsive, by no means always wise, capable indeed of tremendous miscalculations and mistakes. He is just the son of Jonas, the homely "pilot of the Galilean lake." The heart in his bosom is warm and eager; but it is a common human heart, and it is far from a sinless one. Upon it, this very morning, lies, with an indescribable shame and pain, the recent memory of its most dreadful failure; that scene around another fire of coals, when a horrible bewilderment of great fear, an abject terror for his mere mortal life, possessed him, and his own ears heard his own mouth call heaven and earth to witness that he knew absolutely nothing of Jesus the Nazarene.

Such is the second party. Of this man the Other is asking, Do you love Me?

Now let us for the time put aside *the answer* to the inquiry. I do not propose here to study, to dis-

* I quote the phrase from a well-remembered sermon by the late Master of Trinity College, Cambridge, Dr. W. H. Thompson.

cuss, St. Peter's language or St. Peter's feeling as indicated by St. John. I ask to concentrate our attention altogether upon *the question*, as asked—not by anyone, but by Jesus Christ, who had died and risen again, and who sate there now in His tranquil majesty.

Not that I forget the fact that it is a question, and expects an answer. No; I wish, above all things, to prepare for the answer, and that not only as it shall be given by Peter in the Gospel narrative, but as "this same Jesus," who lives to-day and is present in our assembly here, shall hear it spoken to Him by our own human hearts. But for that very purpose let us contemplate *the question*.

"Lovest thou Me?" How does this sound, as regards the thought, the purpose, that lies behind it? What does it say about *the Speaker?* Perhaps it carries with it at first, in our apprehension of it, the air of a demand—a claim, the levy of a due, the summons for an unpaid debt. Here is One who knows (for He knows all things, and this assuredly is a fact present to His mind) that the son of Jonas is under immeasurable obligations to Him, and *ought* to love Him. Most certainly Jesus, for Simon, has done and borne incalculably much within the last few wonderful weeks; Simon is infinitely and for ever the better for the Cross and Passion. And behind all, behind the atoning death, and the sin-covering merit, and the robe of righteousness, and the resultant pardon and peace for this very guilty man—behind it, and above it, there lies all that is implied by the fact that Christ has not only saved Peter, but first made him. He can claim the man's whole being in the double name of Rescuer and of Creator.

Yes, all this is the very truth—truth for me and for you, as much altogether as for that Galilean penitent of old. But I do not think that we read aright the thought and accent of the Lord in His question, Do you love Me? if we read into it this notion—the exaction of a right, the reminder of a debt. He who knew the human heart perfectly (for He has Himself a perfect human heart) would not make so profound a mistake as to cast the demand for payment into the form of an inquiry about love. We mortals and sinners may make such mistakes. There are those, no doubt, who blindly seek to claim, merely as a due, the affection, for example, of a child, the affection being regarded as so much return due for so much care, or as so much honor due to so sacred a relation. But Jesus Christ knew well that human love, while it is possible and sometimes amply right to state the theory of it in terms of duty, can never be *asked for,* face to face, except as just the free response to love; the return, the repercussion, of a tenderness that has first gone freely out as the unselfish gift of the asker's heart.

Just this is the beauty, the glory, the magnetic virtue, once it is apprehended, of the Lord Jesus Christ's inquiry of us, Do you love Me? It is the very touch which lifts the veil from the heart, not of Peter, but of Jesus. In the very act of asking about Peter's love for Him He discloses His love for Peter—a love which is something infinitely different from mere compassion, or mere benevolence, or mere condescension. For it is a love which goes out towards Peter so powerfully, so longingly, with such contact and embrace, that *it cannot rest* without the responsive gaze and clasp of Peter's love to Jesus. The Lord is not just stooping to say, "It is your privilege to love Me." *He covets* His sinful disciple's love; He wants it; it is important to Him; it is much to Him, because He loves the man with such mighty love Himself.

What parent here does not understand it? When your little child first said, in the sweet broken syllables of childhood, "I love you," what did you feel? That your rights were recognized so fitly and so early? That filial and parental relations were already on a proper footing? You felt joy, and the purest thing that can possibly be called pride; for your mighty love to your child made its dawning love to you indescribably great and important, and the more so the more utterly unforced. Someone has dared to apply to our Redeemer that very thought, with a truth great as the simplicity of the words:

> "The little weary lambs
> He gently beareth,
> And on His breast their love
> He *proudly* weareth."

Yes, Jesus Christ cannot ask if Peter loves Him, and cannot ask, as He does today, if *we* love Him, without betraying how much, how really, how strongly, He loves us.

As I said just now, let us in this aspect of the matter put aside the answer, and contemplate the question, that is to say, the Questioner.

Oh, human soul, here before God to-day, listen to the inquiry of Jesus Christ, and give yourself time to understand what it means about Himself.

Are you acquainted with grief, perhaps such grief —so long and deep—that it has seemed at last rather to benumb the heart than pierce it, yet leaving the consciousness of loss, of solitude, of change, only too complete? Nevertheless, One stands beside you who covets the love of your maimed and almost paralyzed spirit. He would be so delighted to have it! For He greatly loves you. And listen, He is asking, and it is for that very reason that He is asking—Do you love Me?

He is acquainted with grief Himself, in depths which He has sounded alone. The woe is over for Him, but not the experience: *"Souffrir passe; avoir souffert demeure éternellement."* He understands you, as sorrow understands sorrow; but He also loves you, and He is avaricious of your love. Let Him have it, Him the eternal Truth and Beauty, but also the Brother and the Friend. And when your love has met and satisfied His, believe me, there shall take place a miracle at the point of contact "your sorrow shall be turned into joy."

Human heart, distracted, bewildered, preoccupied with we know not what—dissatisfied, perhaps, apart from Christ; perhaps, far sadder still, satisfied for the time apart from Him—to-day let no word be spoken by me of the vast truths which concern duty, law, and judgment to come. It shall be enough this hour to say once more, Listen to the asking Christ. Behold the Son of God! Behold the Man of men! You are profoundly important to Him. He wants, He covets you; He will "proudly wear" your love; He is asking whether it is for Him. Let your heart meet His, and for you too the contact shall work miracles; life shall be life to you now indeed, temptations shall be trodden down beneath you, pure joys all made purer, every purpose lifted, every trial dignified, and "life and death and then that vast for ever," shall be attuned, by the magic of His sacred love, into "one grand sweet song."

"That ye may know the love of Christ which passeth knowledge."

"Lovest thou Me?" O Love, that lovest me so much as to ask the question, Thou knowest that I love Thee!

XI

THE HOLY SPIRIT AND THE LOVE OF GOD

A Whitsunday Sermon

"The love of God is shed abroad in our hearts, by the Holy Ghost which is given unto us."—Rom. v. 5.

Somewhat more literally we may read: "The love of God has been poured out in our hearts, by means of the Holy Ghost which was given to us."

There is a divine simplicity about these words. They speak of immense mysteries; of God and of His inmost love, of the eternal Spirit and His inscrutable workings, and of what is a mystery only less in order than the things divine—our human heart. But the words which touch and indicate these unfathonable things are the simplest possible. Every one of them belongs to the plainest of plain English; the longest of them is but a dissyllable. And this is no rare phenomenon in the heavenly Book. Again and again the Bible speaks its plainest just when it is leading us into the inner sanctuaries of truth. It is full of truths which we cannot possibly "find out unto perfection." But it speaks as if it would tell us all about them that it can, all that we can apprehend to our blessing. The falsely mysterious, which delights in "great swelling words," has no place in the Bible.

Let us approach our text, and interrogate it. In this its divine simplicity, what is it saying to us to-day, on this great Sunday of the Spirit? We will seek our answer under two or three special titles.

i. *"The Love of God":* that is to say, the love felt by God towards man, the personal affection of the Almighty. Some have seen in the words another and opposite reference, as if the Apostle meant our love for God, our love of God, as an emotion generated, or liberated, in our hearts by the Holy Spirit. And some, more mystically, have read in our text the thought that the Spirit's work is to infuse and diffuse within us the eternal Love itself in such a sense that it becomes, as it were, our own, and returns to its source in the incense of our surrender to God, our delight and rest in Him. But the context (verse 8) surely gives a decisive answer in favor of the simplest, while most wonderful, of the reference: "God commendeth *His Love toward us,* in that while we were yet sinners Christ died for us." That verse stands in close logical connection with this, and the reference must be the same.

"The Love of God," then, His "marvelous loving-kindness," as the Psalmist has it;* the tenderness and endearment of Him who is Love, towards us sinners, toward us who have fled from ourselves to Him and "laid hold on His strength and made peace with Him" in His own way—this is the particular reference here of "the love of God." It is the kindness of the eternal Heart towards those who believe, towards the Lord's own, "the children of men who put their trust" in the deep "shadow of His wings."

Abundantly true it is that the Scriptures speak, amply, magnificently, of a love of God which is over all His works. "God loved the world," and "*so*" loved it—not the Church, not the saints, not the chosen, but the world. With the love of an infinitely "faithful Creator,"† He loved, and loves, the world, and from that love flows the whole tide of benignant providence and all the sweetness of the message of the Gospel to "whosoever will." But this glorious exterior circle leaves undimmed to our view in Scripture the "glory that excelleth," the inner circle, the love of the Lord for His own, His ransomed, His saved, "the flock of the high heavenly Pastor, Christ" (to use Ridley's almost dying words), those who "hear His voice and follow Him," and whom He "knows by name." This love

---

* Ps. xvii. 7. † 1 Pet. iv. 19.

is peculiar and distinctive, a light in the inner Sanctuary, beaming above the Ark of the better Covenant, within the veil where the Forerunner has gone in.*

The two spheres are in concentric harmony. It is so (if we may illustrate God by man) in human things. Not seldom has been seen the beautiful phenomenon of the philanthropist who is also the ideal father, or ideal mother—a Fowell Buxton, an Elizabeth Fry; a life which to the world is known for its devotion to mankind in large and far-seeing enterprises and sacrifices, but which to the nearer circle is known as the glowing center of home affections and intimate friendships. And can we not think so of the Eternal and Almighty? His universal lovingkindness—this is one thing, and a thing more wide and deep than created thought can measure. But His special, inmost love to His own regenerate children in His own Son—this is another thing, and nearer still to the heart of all life and bliss.

Of this the text is speaking. For the Apostle has just been leading us up, along the golden stairs of his great Epistle, to the peace and joy of those who have obtained salvation. We have traveled by the way of the Cross, by the way of faith, to the wonderful rest of justification, and into the very

* Heb. vi. 19, 20.

righteousness of God. We have heard how those who believe possess peace with Him, and rejoice in Him, and in the hope of His glory. And these are the persons in view in this text of ours, with its words about "the love of God." It is no vague description, no portrait which may be meant for anyone. It means not all and sundry who pass under the Christian name; would to God that name and thing were so linked together that it could do so! But only those answer the description here who have actually "come" to the personal Redeemer to have life, only those who, by grace, have said "Yes" to grace, and entered into Christ.

Such is the burthen and the bearing of the words. Behold this inner love of God, His family love! "What manner of love hath the Father bestowed" upon that happy circle! It is as free and unbought as mercy can be; for, as St. Paul goes on to say, it first went forth in its tender power when they were "sinners"—yes, when they were "enemies" and "ungodly." But it is as genuine, as warm, as strong and deep, as it is unmerited. The love of the Father for His children of the new birth—behold what it is! "Now are they the sons of God"; and hereafter, when their Lord, their Elder Brother, shall be manifested, it shall be manifested what they are made for, in the love of God; "they shall be like Him, for they shall see Him as He is."*

ii. "The love of God is *shed abroad,*" or, more literally, *"hath been outpoured," "in our hearts."* The phrase is beautifully vivid. You cannot take it to pieces and analyze it and explain the process, but you can know what it means. To these human hearts of ours, deep in these living, heaving, conscious worlds within, in the very "springs of thought, and will," and affection, there can be somehow granted the view of this love as a fact, the sense and grasp of this love as a possession. It is there, poured out. It is no alien and separable insertion. It is poured out. Like the shower from the soft cloud, like the odor from the flower, it is there; shed abroad, suffused, pervading, changing, beautifying, glorifying all.

Manifestly it was not so once. These hearts were once as little possessed of this wonderful outpouring as the brown field in the year of drought is possessed of the genial rain. The "outpouring" is now within, it is in the depths; but it was from above; "not of yourselves, it is the gift of God."†

Does this view of the matter seem to any of us an unreality, a thing of vision and enthusiasm? Perhaps nothing in your experience corresponds to it as

* 1 John iii. 2. † Eph. ii. 8.

yet. You have never, perhaps, been much disturbed in thought about your relations to God. His general kindliness and benignity, His "world-love," has seemed to you enough, or it seems to you sufficient that you are by baptism a member of the "congregation of the faithful." May you not on that account reckon upon a special form of His general lovingkindness? Well, let us at least ask the question whether such a view of things squares with the message of St. Paul. What he speaks of here is, in his theory of it, a thing open and common, from one point of view, to all believers, to them all and to no other, while from the other point of view it is a "secret of the Lord." It is a thing "outpoured in the heart," in a way infinitely above nature, while perfectly genuine and recognizable in experience. Our text, and the paragraph of which it is a part, are no flourish of unmeaning rhetoric. They point to a divinely-caused change in the soul's knowledge of the love of God. Do they point any of us to a range of facts as yet indeed to us unknown, but which is knowable, and infinitely good to know?

There are those who know. "The secret of the Lord is with them; He has shewn them His covenant."* They may be slow to speak about it, for fear of seeming to proclaim not their Master but

* Ps. xxv. 14.

themselves; but when they *can* rightly speak, they have indeed a secret to disclose. "This I know, thanks to His grace. Once I heard of Him, but did not know Him; I did not, I could not, see or apprehend the love of God. The fact of His love in general, perhaps, I owned; but it was at best a thing of distance and of shadows. Sometimes I wondered, sometimes I asked of others, what it could be like, what was the sensation, the consciousness, the experience, of 'knowing the love of God.' Now I know. Whereas I was blind, now I see; whereas I was insensible to that light and heat, now I love, because He first loved me. My Father's smile is upon me, shining through the Son, who is infinitely dear to Him, and who has joined me to Himself. I had once 'the spirit of bondage, unto fear.' Now I 'cry,' as with the confidence and simplicity of childhood at home, 'Abba, Father.'* Slow or sudden, the change has come, the new life is here. The love of God has been poured out in my heart."

This is no phantom, dream, or poem; it is an experienced possibility. A human soul which yesterday was full of misgivings about God, or paralyzed in indifference to Him, to-day is able to say, with strong and sober certainty, with the clear persuasion of a true sight of Him in Christ Jesus,

* Rom. viii. 15.

"I know whom I have believed"; "He hath loved me and given Himself for me"; "Behold, what manner of love to me!"; "I am persuaded that neither life nor death shall be able to separate me from the love of God, which is in Christ Jesus our Lord."

To-day, as ever, the eternal Friend stands at the door and knocks, that He may come in with that light in His hand, and make the dreary darkness to be day. To-day, as of old, when that door is opened, His entrance brings a wonderful reality of joy: "I will manifest myself to Him."*

iii. Now in order we come to the glory of Whit-Sunday. We name the name of that ever-blessed AGENT by whom, in the heart's depths, this work is done, this love poured out, this Lord revealed and introduced: *"By the Holy Ghost."*

To-day is Pentecost, the memorial of that great hour of the eternal Spirit when He came indeed, and behold, that small primeval Church, in the supernatural strength of the joy of the Lord, the joy which bursts radiant forth from the love of the Lord, arose and shook the world, and brought it such a blessing as it had never known before. To-day the Church spreads out before us, large and full, the truth of God about His Spirit. We are

* Rev. iii. 20; John xiv. 21.

made to hear to-day of His great work of visible and public power, when the wind blew from the very Throne, and the fiery tongues were showered from the Seven Lamps that burn before it. And we are made to hear also, in our appointed Scriptures, of His personal, separate, secret work of heavenly grace in the individual soul; of the Comforter's dealing with the man so that the Father and the Son come to him, and make Their abode with him; of the Spirit's blessed "fruit" of pure and gracious holiness; of the infinite necessity of His special presence in us; for "if any man have not the Spirit of Christ, he is none of His."*

Manifold are His gifts, His works. Vast indeed is the importance to our life and peace of clear views of what He is. It is blessed to know that indeed it is HE, not only it; that He is no mere gale of power, no mysterious "somewhat" of effluence and influence, but the personal Friend and Lord, coming to His temples,† to bless them with His own loving gifts of life, of purity, of power. But for this one time of meditation take this one sacred fact about Him, this one side and aspect of the mighty range of His glory and His operation. Think of Him as the eternal personal Worker and *Teacher*,

---

* See John xiv., Acts ii., Rom. viii., Gal. v.
† 1 Cor. vi. 19.

understanding, handling, penetrating, knowing His own way in that heart of yours, and taking His own way to bless it. Recollect Him as somehow able, in His personal action, to make the cold, indifferent, sinful soul see, and apprehend, and know, and embrace, and answer to, the love of God—the inner love of God. Remember Him as personally able to manipulate that once rebellious will; sometimes by insensible degrees, sometimes by decisive convictions and a crisis of change memorable to you for ever and ever. Behold Him; He is the Convincer, bringing home to us—home, indeed—"sin and righteousness and judgment." He is the Revealer; He unveils Christ, He explains Him and glorifies Him, and applies Him as vital balm to the aching spirit, which in the reality of its "exceeding need" applies itself to Christ. Then does the man, this man of like passions with us, receive in his heart the effusion of the eternal Love. He knows it, and believes it.* The pardon, the more than pardon, he knows it now; it is a fact; for Jesus Christ is a fact indeed to him. He sees with a new intuition now something of his Lord's glorious beauty. He finds in genuine operation the power of his Lord's presence in him, its power to subdue iniquity, to annul the tempter's besetting strength, to make it sweet and

* John iv. 16.

pleasant to do "from the soul" the will of God; studying to please Him who, in His astonishing love, cares that we sinners should love Him. Yes, the Spirit works, deep at the center, and so Christ, in whom is the whole love of God, becomes there "a living, bright reality," a joy unspeakable, the Secret of the eternal Heart.

iv. "The Holy Ghost *which was given unto us.*" "Given!" Let us note that word as we close. He is indeed a Gift, "the Gift unspeakable," the Gift of God. Here is no mere evolution from within, nor assimilation from around; He is the Gift from above. "From the height above all measure" must "the gracious show descend"; not otherwise can this knowledge of the eternal Love be won by these happy ones, these temples of the Spirit.

And may we also, such as we are, such as we know ourselves to be, share the inestimable boon? Is it not for the *élite,* the aristocracy, of holiness, for apostles, prophets, martyrs, solitaries, heroes? No, no; it is "not according to our works." It is without such miserable price and money as man can pay. It is on a better condition—"according to His abundant mercy," and "for every one that asketh." "For if we, being evil, give," as we delight to do, "good gifts to our children, how much more shall our heavenly Father give His Holy Spirit—to them that ask Him?"

XII

THE ANGEL'S VISIT

Preached at Keswick, before a Congregation of Ministers of Religion

"I am Gabriel, that stand in the presence of God, and I am sent to speak unto thee."—LUKE i, 19.

HERE is the utterance of an Angel, a voice of personal consciousness and experience from another order of being than our own. But we men continually pray, as our Master has bid us do, that the will of God may be done on earth "as it is done in heaven." Then many a priceless lesson for Christian life and labor in general, and for the work of the Christian Ministry in particular, may be rightly drawn from what the holy Book reveals to us of the Angels, of their life, their conduct, their attitude of thought and will, what they are, and what they know themselves to be.

This short sentence, our text, is a case in point. Here comes an Angel from before the eternal Throne to speak with Zacharias in the sanctuary on earth. The man, awe-stricken, amazed, bewildered, falters a request to his Visitor to produce, as it were, his credentials, to give assurance of the reality of his

THE ANGEL'S VISIT.

presence and the validity of his message. And the reply is as we have read: "I am Gabriel, that stand in the presence of God, and I am sent to speak to thee."

In every part of this utterance there is something which meets the heart of the human minister of our Lord Jesus Christ, and reminds him of essential principles of ministerial life and function. May He, who is Master at once of us and of "our elder brethren of the sky," speak to us articulately of these things in the soul, as we study this sentence, spoken on earth, yet from another world.

We might dwell awhile upon the Angel's utterance of his own personal name, *Gabriel, God's Man:* "I am Gabriel"; listening with wondering interest to this avowal that the voice comes from a personality, an Ego, conscious, and willing, and denominated personally, and that the speaker is in intimate and living relations with a personal Supreme, our God and his. But let us pass on at once (remarking this merely by the way) to Gabriel's account of his serving life, and of its inner secrets, and of its issues in action for his Lord. And herein first note the words: *"I stand in the presence of God."*

My brethren of the holy Ministry, here is indeed a motto, a legend, for our ministerial lives. "I stand in the presence of God." Observe the import of each phrase.

i. *"In the presence of God."* The existence of the great Angel was, and is, an existence in the Presence, in the secret of the Presence. He was what he was, as abiding there, as knowing face to face his eternal King, his Maker, Master, All. You know possibly a singularly beautiful hymn, given to us by the pen, or rather through the illuminated soul, of a gifted Indian lady, Miss Ellen Goreh; a hymn beginning,

"In the secret of His Presence
How my soul delights to hide!"

a hymn which may well be a hidden treasure in the memory of every minister of Christ. Now, the truth sung of in that hymn forms the law of the angelic life, of the will and work of a Gabriel. Would we do the eternal Will on earth as it is done by Gabriel in heaven? "In the presence of God" must be our motto, not for times and places only which we call sacred; no, "it is very meet, right, and our bounden duty that we should at all times, and in all places," abide in the Presence, "dwelling with the King, for His work."

ii. But observe again. The blessed Hierarch does not only *exist* "in the presence of God." Listen to him: "I *stand* in the Presence." It is a noteworthy stroke in this bright, sudden picture of celestial life. In that Presence, undoubtedly, he rests, in the sense of unutterable content, and walks, in the sense of perfect internal freedom, and dwells, in the sense of being eternally and inalienably at home. But the fact which is above all present to his ethereal consciousness is this: "I *stand* in the Presence."

Here is the attitude of the Servant. He is profoundly intimate with the Master of his being; he is admitted to, he is conversant with, the *Sanctum,* yea, the *Sanctum Sanctorum;* he treads not the outer court only of the Unseen, but its Holy Place; he does not "sit in the King's gate" only, he "sees the King's face" in the King's innermost chamber. But, therefore, because it *is* the inmost place, and not the outermost, because in a sense so divinely special *the King is there,* therefore, while the Master sits, the servant stands.

Such is the law of the blessed life of this immortal messenger of God. Wherever he is, locally, as we conceive locality, whether "in heaven" itself, whether "caused to fly swiftly" to Daniel at the Persian court,* whether at Jerusalem on his errand to Zacharias, or at Nazareth on that surpassing errand to Mary—always, "in spirit," he is "standing in the presence of God."

* Dan. ix. 21.

THE ANGEL'S VISIT.

We too must be there, and we too must there be standing. Never, by the grace of our Master, let us really forget, let us really quit, that spiritual attitude, the position of the servant who stands, whatever, from other points of view, may be our blessed privileges of liberty and of holy rest.

For Gabriel that standing attitude is immortally lasting and the same. Nineteen ages have rolled away since that hour of incense in the Temple; but his station is the same. To-day, as then, Gabriel is personally the same, the same "I" that spoke its consciousness and its name to the wondering priest; and to-day, as then, he is standing, upright and unwearied, in the Presence. And *we*, too, are never, yes, truly never, to be released from our "standing" there, from our attitude as the servants, the servants *ready for orders and action,* who "see the King's face," attentive to His Will. Never are we to cease so to "stand" on earth, and never in the coming life of heaven.

> "For He hath met our longing
> With words of golden tone,
> That we shall 'serve for ever'
> Himself, Himself alone—
> Shall serve Him, and for ever.
> O hope most sure, most fair,
> The perfect love outpouring
> In perfect service there."*

---

* Miss Havergal.

THE ANGEL'S VISIT. 193

Let us look up to Him who "is able to make us stand," that this "law may be written in our hearts"; that this may lie deep among the inmost secrets of our ministerial will and work. "*I stand* in the Presence."

iii. But Gabriel has more to say: "*And I am sent to speak unto thee.*"

"*I am sent.*" It is not my purpose to-day to discourse upon the principles and the warrant of ministerial commission, in the sense of ministerial authority. Let me rather address myself to what is, after all, the supremely important matter for the soul of the minister himself—to the ministerial commission as it suggests the thought of our subjection, our servitude, to Another; of our being but means and implements, yea, of our being in ourselves "nothing, nothing," apart from the Sender of His servants.

"*I am sent,*" says the great Angel; not merely, "I come," "I am here," but, "*I am sent.*" I stand in the Presence, a servant there. I have indeed such an open vision of my Master's face as makes me, in indescribable reality, His friend. But none the less I am, eternally and absolutely, His servant; and now, in regard to thee whom I address, I come to thee simply as His servant, His servant sent upon His work. My message is not what I have thought fit to bring; I am enjoined to bring it. I have not come to lord it over thee, and to impose myself on thee; I am thy fellow-servant, and to thee, *ex aequo,* I am sent.

The Angel's words in the sanctuary at Jerusalem recall to me certain words, spoken in a very different scene, and by a mortal speaker; they are found in Genesis xxiv. That episode of the divine Book, self-evidential of its own veracity and historicity, by its union of minutely acurate "local color" with a majestic moral simplicity, presents us with "Abraham's servant," illustrious personage among the goodly company of the saintly servants of Scripture. We see him, this Eliezer (for we will take it for granted that this is Eliezer of Damascus), the honored and honorable confidant of that memorable master, who talks with him as with a friend in God, and sends him on his errand graced with so much equipage and dignity that the high-born Rebekah, at the well, accosts him, in the fine natural courtesy of the East, as some great one: "Drink, my lord." He is received into the house at Haran with distinguished attention, and respectfully questioned about his errand to his hosts. And then he speaks, introducing himself with the quiet dignity of one who cares to seem only what he is: "I am Abraham's servant, Abraham's *ebhed,* δοῦλος,—, bondman." Yes, that is what he is. Abraham had either actually purchased him, or he was the son of one whom Abraham had purchased; "born in his house." Under conditions of society then permitted by God, he was Abraham's chattel, his piece of property, and he said that it was so. This man of noble heart and personal dignity, dignified by the intimacy and confidence of the Friend of God, his master, able to enter into the conceptions and purposes of an Abraham, drinking deep of Abraham's spirit of faith and patience—all that this man cares to say of himself is this, "I am Abraham's bond-servant, and I am sent." He was not on his own business, but his master's. So far from seeking his own, he was (may we not say, looking at Gen. xv. 3?) actually taking measures to shut himself out of a wealth which might otherwise have been his inheritance. It mattered not. He belonged; he was not his own. "I am Abraham's servant."

This is a noble picture; I know none fairer of its kind, even in the Scriptures themselves. But is it not more than noble? Is it not written for our learning? It is assuredly for us, who, in a sense so special and so merciful, are called to be the servants of the Eternal Friend of Abraham. It is for us, to lay it upon us ministers of God and of His Word that we never, no, never, pass ourselves off to those whom we approach as anything but the bond-servants of

Christ, and therefore "ourselves their bond-servants, for His sake."*

But Gabriel still stands by the golden altar and the incense-cloud, and speaks to the old priest there. Listen to him again with all the heart. Again let him say the words, in our hearing, and for us: "I stand in the presence of God, and I am sent." Every syllable is instinct with the spirit which forgets the self of the servant in the peace and gladness of the heavenly service. The Angel lives, not unto himself, but unto Him whose face he sees, and whose will he serves for ever.

We do not conceive of the angelic life as a life stunted and confined, unsatisfied and ill at ease. We think of it, and rightly—for such is the indication of the divine Scriptures—as a life that "excels in strength,"† and whose course and tenor is a song of mighty joy. Yes, but none the less (we should instantly say "all the more," were the whole conditions of happiness better understood by us), its law is an absolute subservience to the will and glory of God; an eternal standing in the Presence, a ceaseless going forth on the work to which the great Master sends, and this in order to do and to say what shall bring honor, not to the servant, but to his King. The elect Angels, as by a sacred necessity of

*2 Cor. iv. 5.   † Ps. ciii. 20.

THE ANGEL'S VISIT.

their nature and its bliss, shrink back from glory and worship paid to themselves. If not Gabriel himself, it was a true brother of his heavenly family who said, when the entranced Apostle fell at his feet, "See thou do it not, for I am thy fellow-servant."*

There is very little risk that any of our hearers, any of our neighbors, should fall at our feet to worship us. But there is more than a little risk—such is the human heart in the breast of the human minister—that we may, at the least invitation of human applause, or even of human kindness, fall down and worship ourselves. You know well what I mean; the subtle temptations to self-praise, to self-esteem, to an appropriation to ourselves of an applause which is our Lord's alone, which can spring from almost nothing—when the man is off his guard. But by the grace of Him "whose we are and whom we serve," by that immeasurable grace which can possess even us, it shall not be. We will, in watchful faith, entrust it to His power that it shall not be; that in this thing also, by His power working in us, His will shall be done in us on earth as it is done in heaven.

Our work of ministry brings us often weariness, and sometimes, if we are found faithful, it brings us reproach. But does it not also, if in any degree at

* Rev. xxii 9.

all we are enabled to work for our Lord and in Him, bring us also surprising gifts, ever and anon, of allowance and of kindness from the brethren to whom we minister? Yes; and in view of all this we now humbly resolve, as in His presence, as standing there, and sent only from thence, that whatever henceforth of acceptance, or commendation, or affection, shall come to us as ministers of Jesus Christ, it shall not be fuel for the flame of self; it shall be "henceforth no longer for ourselves, but for Him who died for us, and rose again." The tribute shall not be slipped into our own purse, for that is theft; it shall be passed on at once to the Master to whom it belongs, for we belong to Him. We will accept no secret and surreptitious bounties behind His back.

I say this, my brethren, as myself desiring to hear it, and as knowing that it will be welcome to your hearts, taught by the Holy Ghost. It shall be so. We too, like those who serve above, are called to stand in the Presence. We too are nothing if not the purchased bond-servants of the heavenly Abraham. And as such we will appropriate no contributions to self-complacency in our work for our Master, not even from our Master's friends. As His, we are outside of it, we are above it, we are beyond it. What He has given to us to be, to have, to hold for Him, we will now and evermore be passing on and giving back at once to Him whose only right it is.

So I leave this utterance of the Angel's voice upon our souls for our guidance, strength, and peace, by the grace of our Lord and King. Be it henceforth, more than ever yet, the inmost thought of each pastoral heart: "I am the servant of Jesus Christ; in His presence, standing in His presence, sent from His presence, yet sent *in* His presence still. I am nothing outside this. And I come, O men and brethren, to you as a man who is not your master, but only sent, '*under* athority,' from my Master, to speak to you, to serve you. I present myself before you in all my pastoral life, in public, in society, in private, in the Church, in the home, everywhere and always, not as your oracle, not as your spiritual chief, not as your lecturer, not as your speculative philosopher, but as your fellow-servant, who has come to bring you a message from One who is absolute for me, and absolute for you."

It is an ideal of the pastoral spirit which is unspeakably searching, certainly as applied to the preacher's own heart; and to the end of our chapter we shall need to cry: "Enter not into judgment with *Thy servant.*" But it is an ideal which we are overwhelmingly bound to set before our eyes and bind upon our hearts. And it is an ideal which (not to our glory), may be, and shall be, *indefinitely* brought toward realization, as we welcome into our abased spirits the fulness of the Holy One.

XIII

THE MINISTRY OF THE NEW COVENANT

Preached at an Ordination in the Cathedral, Liverpool.

"Who also hath made us able ministers of the New Covenant."—2 COR. iii. 6.

SOME words are necessary, as we approach the message of this text, by way of reminder of its context and exposition of its phrase.

First, *the context*. The verse forms part of that wonderful discourse concerning the trials, toils, strength, and glory, of Ministry for Christ, which occupies the opening chapters of this great Epistle: a passage in which nothing is said about the exterior of the thing, about gradations and subordinations of rank, about divisions of labor and of honor; but in which everything is said about the sacred interior of all true ministration, about the spiritual relations of the minister to the Lord, and to the flock, and to the Gospel, and to himself.

Read these pages, honored brethren in Christ, about to be admitted by the Church, as "the called ones of Jesus Christ," to His definitely commissioned service; read them, and mark them, and inwardly digest them, by day and by night. If you want searching (and we always want it), they will search you through the soul. If you want solemnizing and spiritualizing, if you want to be lifted out of the desert of a mere officialism and routine into the paradise of a life lived and a work wrought in God, they will shew you how this can be. If you want reanimation of soul about your coming rest, and crown, and glory, about the faithful minister's blessed prospects in death and in eternity, here you will hear indeed a voice from heaven. Lastly, if you want a new definition and affirmation to you of your message, of your Gospel, of what you go out into church, and mission-room, and street, and lane, and parlor, and loft, and cellar, to report, and testify, and teach, you will find it here, you will find it in my text.

Immediately, the text is prefaced* by a confession of man's personal incapacity for the ministry of Christ. "We are not sufficient of ourselves to think anything as of ourselves," "to reason out anything, as from ourselves." He does not mean that we are imbeciles in intelligence, that we are to abjure the use of mind. The thought is that we are wholly incapable of originating a Gospel, or of amending one; of evolving a message out of our own con-

* Verse 5.

sciousness; of speculating out a Christianity; of telling any man out of our own heads how the ruin of his nature is to be repaired, and the burthen of his guilt to be lifted off, how he is to find strength and power to have victory over the devil, the world, and self, how he is "to glorify God on earth, and to enjoy Him fully for ever." He means that we cannot *excogitate* answers to these things, as we could in the case, for instance, of many questions of political or of physical science. We are by nature dumb and blind before the problems of salvation, before the mystery of guilt and of spiritual impotence. To know what to think about these things, and what to say, is far above our own reach.

But then (the Apostle unfolds this also), we are not below the reach of Him who can enable us to know. He "hath made us able." He hath qualified us, capacitated us, for His work. Sovereign in skill and power, He has taken us from the dust and ruins of the Fall, and from the thick darkness of our ignorance of Him; has made us what He requires as His instruments, and has taught us what we require for His Message. With a *fiat* as creative as that in Genesis, He "hath shined in our hearts,"* and revealed to us the glory of the sinner's Saviour and the saint's Head. He has quickened us from

* Chap. iv. 6.

the death of sin to the life which is hid with Christ in God. He has shewn to us, and given to us, His Son. He has shewn to us, and entrusted to us, His Gospel.* So, we are able. We know our Master, our message, and our strength.

One word, and one only, on the phraseology of the text. I have ventured to read "new covenant" in place of the "new testament" of the Authorized Version. It is not lightly I do so. But I conceive that the word διαθήκη, in every place, or almost every place, of its occurrence in the New Testament, answers better, both by usage and by context, to the idea of a covenant than to the more limited idea of a testamentary will. So I render: "He hath made us able, competent, ministers of the NEW COVENANT."

I have spent some time in preface. But in this case the preface is vital to the application, and has already been conveying it in part. For we have seen already something of the incapacity of man to be a minister; of his profound insufficiency, ἀφ' ἑαυτοῦ, to think out a Gospel; aye, and so to enter with his soul into the Gospel, even when externally revealed, as to teach it with living power, till a grace which is altogether from above has "shined in his heart" and shown to him Jesus Christ. And we have

* Chap. iv. 7.

seen, in the example of the Apostle and his coworkers, what that grace can do. It can make the blind see; it can make the weak strong; it can make the dead live; it can *"make us able."*

My brethren in the ministry of our Lord Jesus Christ, after the ancient and holy order of the Church of England, this is the first message of the text to you and to your preacher: "We are not sufficient; but He hath made us able." You, Presbyters and Deacons just about to be, you all have to be, above all things, *this* in your ministration—ministers of a message. And you are not sufficient for it. And He, if you are as you say, hath made you able. I weigh my words when I call you *all* "ministers of a message." I do not forget that the duty of the Deacon differs from that of the Presbyter, in this respect among others, that while the Presbyter is, as such, a commissioned minister of the divine Word, the Deacon is so only by special grant. But in the broad facts of actual Church life I see this line of distinction greatly modified by inexorable circumstances. So I freely address you all as distinctively ministers of the Word, and bid you remember how the Reformed Church of England, "from the first compiling of her public liturgy" to this day, has put that Word and its ministration in the full foreground. There it stands in her plan of worship as described in the "Prefaces," and in the examples of preaching presented in the Homilies, and in the whole drift and burthen of this Office of Ordination in which we are engaged to-day. You are many things besides ministers of holy order, stewards and dispensers of divine Sacraments. Yes, but still, in the view of our mother Church, expressed in her own authentic utterances, such is the supreme importance of your work about the Word of God that you are nothing if not messengers, nothing if not witnesses of the revealed and unaltered Gospel of our Lord Jesus Christ, the New Covenant in His Name.

And oh, you are "not sufficient," brethren, "not sufficient to think anything," not sufficient therefore to preach anything, "as of yourselves."

Minister of Jesus Christ, are you setting out to-day light-heartedly on your work? Are you assured that you are the heir of all the ages, confident that you are a guide of the blind, satisfied perhaps that old ways, views, and words have had their day, and that you and your generation, by a few bold strokes of accommodation, by the casting overboard of a little more of the supernatural, by a little more explanation-away of such stubborn words as "sin," and "guilt," and "law," and "propitiation," and "new heart," by a somewhat extended excursion on the "down-grade" of religious liberalism, will bring man and Christianity to terms? Or are you trusting to do your clerical work, in its philanthropic aspects, so well, and vigorously, and sympathetically, that there will be little need for doctrines, broad or narrow, while you educate, amuse, and befriend your people into Christian virtue? Recur in time to the Apostle's words, in view of the work, as he at least understood it: "Not that we are sufficient of ourselves to think anything as from ourselves; but our sufficiency is of God." You have to deal for God with man—fallen, rebel, sinful man, "dead in trespasses and sins." How to repair *that* ruin is a secret known to God alone. As regards the answer to *that* problem, you must not, you dare not, deviate from His judgment in your estimate, from His revelation in your scheme, from his Word in your message. The modern world can, if it will, bandy about the mysteries of the faith from magazine to magazine, between installments of serial fiction. The Apostle, who had seen Jesus Christ, said, "We are not sufficient to think anything as from ourselves; our sufficiency is of God."

Happy is the intending minister of Christ who in *this* respect has lost confidence in himself. Blessed is the man that thus *"feareth always."* Bright are the ministerial prospects of him who has come to that most reasonable of conclusions, that his message must be humbly learnt at the feet of the Lord and His Apostles, and must be lovingly and faithfully delivered in the presence and in the peace of his Master—as message, not as speculation, nor as rhapsody; as message first, whatever else it be.

Are you, in the Christian poet's words, thus "confident in self-despair"? Then you are getting hold of your "sufficiency." You are learning the infinity of your need, and that is the straight way to getting into contact with the infinity of the Lord's supply.

Let us resolve boldly thus to "fear always." It is the sort of fear that does not shrink, but clings. It does not bury "that one talent which is death to hide," but it takes its Owner's advice every day how to lay it out. It fears because of adoring love. It fears not lest it should be true to Him. It cannot bear not to glorify His beloved, His blessed Name.

Fear always thus. It will drive you to trust always. It will keep you close to the fountain-head of power and peace. It will constrain you to walk with God. And the ministry which has not at the back of it a walk with God may have a name, may have a fame, to live, yet it is dead.

But of what in particular does the Apostle say that we are "made able" to be ministers? "Able minister of the NEW COVANANT; not of the letter, but of the Spirit; for the letter killeth, but the Spirit giveth life." You consult the context about the meaning of this "letter" and this "Spirit"; and you find that the letter means the holy Law, immovable, graven in the rock for ever, and divinely fatal to the sinner's hopes if he would use it as his title to life; and you find that the Spirit means the Holy Spirit, here named as the crowning and concentrating blessing of the Gospel of our Lord Jesus Christ. "We preach not," he means, "as our distinctive message, the sacred, the divine anathema; we preach Him who has taken it on His own immaculate head, and, in the infinite merit of that sacrifice, now sheds into awakened man's inmost being the Holy Ghost, the Lord, the Life-Giver, to make the new heart, to teach the art and practice of new and saving trust, to sustain in the new life, to prompt the new song, to unfold the new Covenant, to make all things new from the inmost to the outmost of the man."

Now observe—all this is called the NEW COVENANT ($\dot{\eta}$ καινὴ διαθήκη). I beg you to attend to that word. It is out of the fashion of current religious thought; not often does the modern preacher discourse upon the Covenant. The word is strict and definite; and too often now the drift even of evangelistic religion is toward the vague, the fluid, and the lax. But there stands the word in the Book of God, large and prominent. And as I pause and ponder it, lo! out of its rugged strictness and severity begin to spring ideas of life, and love, and glory. I begin to see in it precious and splendid intimations of a plan, a compact, an agreement, for the blessing of believing man, "ordered in all things and sure," deeds and seals valid for ever in the eternal Court, oaths and promises to which the ancient hills are fleeting and unsubstantial things. I draw nearer, and I study deeper, and I see in this New Covenant a thing whose settlement and security lie between the Father and the Son. All its blessings are lodged in the incarnate, sacrificed, and risen Christ, its Mediator and Surety, lodged in Him for me, because for all who come to God by Him. His covenanted joys and treasures are mine in Him, and, because covenanted, sure and certain; no fortuitous largess, so to speak, of a precarious bounty, but possessions ready sealed, and delivered over to the entitled applicant with the majestic precision of the long-matured determinations and vast securities of celestial law. I ponder the word, I ponder the thing, of which I am enabled to be the minister; and it glows within my own soul as a living treasure for my own profoundest needs. It is indeed a word of rock, but its material is the "Rock of ages, cleft for me"; cleft for my hiding-place,* whence I may watch His goodness, and where the outskirts of His glory may pass before me; cleft for the issuing into me of the eternal waters of the overflowing Spirit, the Spirit of the Son of God, "which they that believe in Him do receive."†

"The NEW COVENANT." Let us be very definite about it, for so the Scriptures are. Do you want a *locus classicus* upon the subject? You have it, amongst other places, in Heb. x. 16, 17: "This is the covenant that I will make with them"—with them that are sanctified, separated to God, by the one Offering of Calvary: "I will put My laws into their hearts, and in their minds will I write them; and their sins and iniquities will I remember no more." And as we turn to the fontal passage in Jeremiah (xxxi. 33, 34), we find, as you know, that the order of thought reverses that of mention. *First,* blessed be God, is the present and abundant pardon, the sure and covenanted acceptance, for the great Mediator's solitary sake. *Then,* as a gift equally of sovereign grace, and to be received with equal simplicity *in* Him, is the writing of the laws—*laws* as much as ever, strong and binding as on the tablets of Sinai, but written now upon the heart, the thought,

* Exod. xxxiv. 19-23.   † John vii. 39.

the understanding, love, and will, of God's new-born Israelite.

Dear brethren in the Lord, will you accept and put into use what in Jesus Christ is yours—ability, full equipment, to be the living ministers of such a Covenant? Will you make plain to men's thoughts its glories, its divine origination, its lodgment in Christ, its fulness and presentness of blessing? Will you plead with men to be reconciled on covenant terms with God? Will you beguile them, will you adjure them, to come "into the bond of the covenant," holding up before them the marvel of the work wrought and the price paid to make it valid, preaching it as "the New Covenant in the Lord's blood, shed for the remission of sins"?* Will you dilate with the emphasis, and interest, and unstudied skill of the messenger who is in love with his message, because it is his own life and joy, upon the magnificent *doubleness* of this Covenant? Will you say strong things, strong as the Word of God, to the true penitent, about a covenanted *acceptance,* large, unreserved, secure, and present: "Their sins and their iniquities will I remember no more"? Will you preach heart-searchingly about sin and the law, and yet, and then, preach also justification by

* See Matt. xxvi. 28, Luke xxii. 20.

faith, peace now with God through our Lord Jesus Christ:

> "Thy tears, not mine, O Christ,
>   Have wept my guilt away";
> "Thy Cross, not mine, O Christ,
>   Has borne the awful load"?

And then will you preach that other limb of the Covenant with equal insight, and decision, and thanksgiving: "I will put My laws into their hearts, and write them in their minds"? Will you make men sure that in the Mediator are treasured both pardon and celestial holiness; that in the Head is lodged for the members life, and more abundant life; that from Him, under covenant security and seal, we are to receive—not generate, but receive—in humblest reliance upon Him, that new nature, that new heart, wrought by the Spirit in the regenerate man, the heart which "loveth righteousness and hateth wickedness," over which sin hath no more dominion, which walketh at liberty, keeping His commandments? Will you make it plain that under this august Covenant there is guaranteed to faith the power of the indwelling and conquering Spirit, by whom Christ dwells within, as truly as there is guaranteed to faith the blissful acceptance of the guilty by reason of the once-offered Blood? Will you evermore enforce on them, and on yourselves, the infinite spirituality of the law, and the perpetual need of the humblest confession of your sins? But will you also, and meanwhile, make it largely and lovingly plain to them that Jesus Christ, through His Spirit, can peacefully empower the heart, by His own saving virtue, to submit itself evermore beneath His hands, that He may write that law upon it, while the heart sings with solemn joy: "Thy commandments are not grievous"; and that all this is under covenant, oath, and seal, and secured for you in the Mediator's hand?

I am sure these views of the Covenant are "as the oracles of God." I solemnly call on you to see if they are not, and, if they are, to resolve that your ministry shall strike no lower key, no weaker melody, nor less perfect harmony. Ponder this great thing in your studies, on your knees, over your Bibles, and in your work for men. Unfold it, as the basis of all the variety of incidental topics, in the sacred pulpit. And when you stand at the Master's Table, make the Covenant indeed the theme of your adoring thanks, and the couch of your happy rest. Ponder the holy Cup in the light of covenant truth. Drink it, and give it, with that truth glowing in your own heart: "This is My blood of the New Covenant"; "This cup is the New Covenant in My blood." He that knows the Covenant, and clasps it, and ministers it, will indeed venerate and love its Seal.

Go forth, in the name of the Son of God, to your ministry of this "everlasting Covenant" made with Him for every one that believeth. Advance to your whole work with all your aims and thoughts simplified into this; that you are set, by grace, upon glorifying God in this ministry of the Covenant. Let me leave that word last upon your souls, that deep, holy, immortal aim, *to glorify God*. "Supernatural is the desire to glorify God," wrote that great saint, Henry Venn the elder, a century ago; "it is the bud and the blossom which brings forth all the fruit the Church of God bears."[*] The Lord lead you forth in peace thus to do His will, in His rest, and in His strength, and for His sake, till you lie down to die into His presence, taking your Master's words, in your humble measure, upon your failing lips: "I have glorified Thee upon the earth; I have finished the work which Thou gavest me to do."

[*] Memoir, p. 14.

XIV.

THE LORD'S BROTHER: THE SON OF GOD

Preached on Trinity Sunday in St. Catharine's College Chapel, Cambridge

"I saw James, the Lord's brother. . . . It pleased God . . . to reveal His Son in me."—GAL. i. 19, 15, 16.

THIS is the Sunday of the Holy Trinity. The seasons of the Church and their teaching have led us, since Advent, through "the days of the flesh" of the Lord Jesus, and up to His Ascent to heaven, and then on to the Descent of the Holy Ghost upon His Church. To-day they culminate in this supreme and eternal truth. We are permitted, as it were, to look through that door in heaven which was opened to St. John in Patmos, and to see the Throne itself, and the living Mystery of infinite while personal Being which shines and reigns upon it. In oneness of Nature, in threeness of eternal inner Relation, behold our GOD! Lo! Father, Son, and Spirit; bright Depth of reciprocal and almighty internal love; immeasurable Fountain of that wonderful outflow, redeeming love; the love that loved the world; "the love of God, which is in Jesus Christ our Lord."

I make no attempt this morning to discourse in order upon the doctrine of the Trinity. But I take occasion from the day to set before you some thoughts akin to the mighty Theme, and meanwhile as closely as possible akin to our hearts and lives. After all, the central splendor of the truth of the Trinity, for us men and our salvation, is our Lord Jesus Christ, God and Man, Man and God. In Him we know the Father: From Him we have the Spirit. Him the Father gives us as His supreme Gift. Him the Spirit glorifies to our hearts as His supreme Theme. He is at once our Door into the heaven of the throne, and the visible Form upon that throne itself, in whom our God is seen.

Let us speak a little, then, of Jesus Christ—Son of Man, therefore Man; Son of God, therefore God.

i. *"I saw James, the Lord's brother."* So St. Paul writes in the first verse of my text. It is a sentence of the simplest and most prosaic matter of fact. Looking back over twenty years or so from the date of his writing, he recalls a certain visit to Jerusalem. It was a visit to Peter, and it lasted just a fortnight. As it happened, he did not meet the other Apostles on that occasion; John and the rest chanced to be out of the way. Only, he did see

James, the Lord's brother. That is all; the subject drops at once.

What a simple note, as from a diary! There is no mystery here, nothing transcendental. It is a mention as natural as if he had said, "I saw Timotheus on such an occasion," or, "I saw Sergius Paulus." But think for a moment what it suggests; reflect upon its witness to the recency and to the absolute reality of the human biography of Jesus Christ. No matter now what exactly was the "brotherhood" between James and the Lord; it was anywise *some* human connection, such as might have subsisted equally well between some other two Palestinian men. As such, this little commonplace allusion to an incident of intercourse carries us right up, beyond all possible myth or legend, to the very birth of Christianity. Here is a man recalling his interview with another man at a time which was much nearer then than the date of my degree is to me now, or the date of my ordination—events which, however, are as vividly present to me as many an occurrence of this year. And this man whom he recalls had shared a home with Jesus, had taken his meals with Him, had very likely sat in the school with Him, and worked with Him in the shop. He would remember very well indeed His look, His voice, His manner, just as I remember "the old familiar faces" of my father's home, or of my college friendships.

Here, then, is the simplest possible fact for our contemplation, from one side. A letter-writer, whose letter betokens him a man of sane, vigorous, and eminently practical character, recalls visits and conversations which brought him across a friend who happened to have been, not long before, a member of a certain home-circle in Northern Palestine. It is a common fact, artlessly told. But then, the wonder of it from another side is just this, that *it is* fact. That home-circle of Galilean Nazareth *was* a then recent fact. And it embraced among other members, two men, called "brothers" all around the town. One was James; the other was—"the Lord!" James was "the Lord's" brother.

ii. This designation arrests us. "The LORD." It is a term reverent and religious. What does it connote about Him who, if James was His brother, was also, and in the same sense, the Brother of James? Let this epistle to Galatia answer the question. Remember, it is a letter which, as I have just said, bespeaks the writer a man not only of keen and critical understanding, but of a large and balanced wisdom. It is a document which carries on its face, in its unselfish jealousy for all that is kind, true, and mutually just and considerate, one of the surest guarantees we can possibly have that it is free from emotional delusion. And its writer, remember, this friend of "James, the Lord's brother," stands not many years from the time when he first met James; as little as James was a myth to him, so little was James' Brother. But James' Brother was nevertheless to him "the LORD," in a sense upon which my other text, and with it the rest of the Epistle, throws the light of eternity itself. Think of such words as the following and imagine them said now of one whose brother you had known at school, or I had known at College: "It pleased God to reveal His Son in me"; "Paul, an Apostle, not by man, but by Jesus Christ, and God the Father, who raised Him from the dead"; "Our Lord, who gave Himself for us, that He might redeem us"; "I am crucified with Christ; Christ liveth in me; I live by faith in the Son of God, who loved me and gave Himself for me"; "Christ hath redeemed us from the curse of the law, being made a curse for us"; "Ye are all one in Christ"; "God sent forth His Son; God hath sent forth the Spirit of His Son into your hearts, crying Abba, Father"; "God forbid that I should glory, save in the Cross of our Lord Jesus Christ"; "In Christ Jesus nothing availeth but a new creation"; "The grace of our Lord Jesus Christ be with your spirit. Amen."

Such, to the view of James' friend, was James' Brother. To Paul, this wonderful Being, who was practically his contemporary in human life, was, on the other hand, Lord, Redeemer, immeasurably more than man, Son of the Eternal, Object of saving faith, mysterious Inhabitant of the heart. To reveal, fully His glories to the soul, God the Father must interpose.* Once seen, once known, He is all in all for the being who has found Him. Into Him a Paul, with all his vast wealth of thought and will, sinks, as it were, delightfully submerged and lost; "I live, yet not I; Christ liveth in me."† He is not called GOD in set terms indeed. But can all this language mean less than Deity? Either James' Brother is also God made Man, or Paul's language about Him is high treason against the Almighty. For it makes out the Brother of James to be man's absolute Master and Possessor, man's inmost Secret of eternal life, man's ultimate and adequate Object of saving trust, man's Grace-Giver, man's all-satisfying joy and glory.

James' Brother; Son of GOD!

I know not whether I carry you with me, but to my own soul, I must avow, this double utterance of the Galatian Letter, written down within thirty years

* Gal. i. 15. † Gal. ii. 20.

of the Crucifixion, speaks with a quite peculiar power about alike the solidity and the glory of the Christian's faith. It takes me up at one step to the very first days of young Christianity, and there it shows me with one hand a rock-surface of personal incidents, seen in the broadest daylight of human life. With the other hand it shows, me, set upon that platform, moving and acting upon it, the splendor of a certainty at once primeval, sober, and divine, that the Jesus of human history is also the Lord of the upper heavens, the mysterious Sacrifice for my sins, the Life of my life, the Master of my will, "strength of my heart, and my portion for ever."

My brethren, when I cast about for a theme on which to address you in this sacred place, on this my first occasion of privilege as a preacher of God's Word in our College, it seemed to me that of all possible choices it must be best to choose the supreme Theme, Jesus Christ. So we have sought to consider Him, simply Him, in the mystery, fact, and glory of what He is.

He has passed before us as Man, our elder Brother, Partner of man's life, Denizen of man's home, cognizant of our whole human circumstances, "able to be touched with the feeling of our infirmities." James' Brother knows all about human conditions, "in all points once tested like as we are, yet without sin"; yes, blessed be His Name! "without sin"; so that to His perfect sympathy is for ever joined the omnipotence to help which, without moral perfectness, could not be. He has passed and shone before us, on the other hand, as the King of Glory, the everlasting Son of the Father, the sinner's Pardon, the disciple's Life and Strength and Purity and blessed Hope beyond.

Behold the MAN! Behold the LORD! "We would see JESUS"—and we may. We would believe on Him to life eternal—and we may. Such a Redeemer, in the infinite nearness of His Manhood, in the infinite fulness of His Deity, comes to meet our asking with open and everlasting arms. Received, believed, obeyed, He gladdens with summer sunshine every corner of our days. He cleanses our very thoughts —bright miracle!—by His presence in the midst of them. He ennobles our every faculty, body and mind, by using it for His will. And at the end—He will not let us "see death"; "we shall see HIM, as HE is."

XV

LIVING STONES

Preached in St. Catharine's College Chapel, Cambridge.
"Ye, also as living stones."—1 Pet. ii. 5.

WE owe to this paragraph of St. Peter's a designation of our Lord priceless in its significance and power. Here, and here only, in Holy Scripture, in the sentence just before the text, He is called the Living Stone. Repeatedly elsewhere, both in the Old Testament and in the New, we read of Him as the Stone, the Rock, Rock of Ages, Stone of the Corner—*Angulare Fundamentum*. And we have indeed abundant Scriptures where He appears in all the glory and in all the power of Life. "I am He that liveth" ὁ ζῶν: nay, "I am the Life."* But here only do the two truths meet in one magnificent witness to His worth and glory; only here is He named "the Living Stone."

It is a pregnant phrase, when the mind attends to it and takes it in. Christ is *the Stone*. The word speaks to us of all that is solid, massive, steadfast, strong. It suggests at once ideas of immovable

*Rev. i. 18; John xi. 25.

principle and ever-persistent purpose, and of capacity at once to resist and to sustain. We read in it how our Master is "the same yesterday and to-day and for ever,"* in a fixity which the cliffs and crags may picture, but to which all the while they are but as fleeting shadows, as unsubstantial dreams, placed beside Him who is "this same Jesus"† for ever and for evermore.

But then, besides, Christ is *the Living* Stone. Taken by itself, the rock-metaphor gives us all we want of certainty and strength; but there is nothing in it of itself to warm the thought and to move the soul to a personal regard. But behold! He is the Living Stone; He is Strength instinct with glowing Life. This foundation, this bulwark, this massy tower, "foursquare to opposition"—look at it again; it is not *it*, but HE. The Rock has voice, and eyes, and arms, and heart. He lives, all over and all through; and it is with a life which pours itself out in thought and sympathy and help and love, to the refugee upon the Rock.

So speaks the Apostle, so by the Apostle speaks the Holy Ghost, of this double glory of Jesus Christ our Lord. But he has more to say, and of the same kind. *The* Living Stone is One. But there are many living stones. *The* Son of God is Only-Be-

*Heb. xiii. 8.   †Acts i. 11.

gotten. But there are many sons of God. Has man, in all his weakness and in all his inner spiritual death, touched Christ? Then the Stone gives man His strength; the Life gives man His life. And the result is a living stone. And such living stones come to be many; and a Hand, mighty to construct as well as mighty to save, takes them, and builds with them. They come together, in their strength and in their life; and the strength is multiplied, and the life flows with stronger and fuller pulses, and lo! there results (to use St. Peter's words here), "a spiritual household, an holy priesthood," "offering to God by Jesus Christ" the mighty sacrifice of a surrender and a service free, conscious, individual *and* magnificently fraternal and combined.

This is a rich and animating ideal, is it not? And, like all true ideals, it is given to us, not for contemplation only, but to be realized, nearer and ever nearer to its perfect truth. Look at it, with purposes as practical as possible, from both its sides. Here is the Christian man as the living stone. Here is the Christian company as the structure of such living stones. The stone precedes the structure in the order of thought; so let us take the stone first, the living stone, the Christian man. What is he to be? What through Christ *can* he be? I emphasize that word, What *can* he be? For St. Peter, obviously, is

LIVING STONES. 227

writing about a thing possible and actual: "You are living stones; you are being builded up as such." It was a fact of human experience for these disciples of the Asiatic Missions, these people recently sunk and sodden in Levantine languor and vice, these helpless slaves of pagan owners, as many of them were besides. They had actually *become to be* living stones. Then we in Cambridge, in England, in Christendom to-day can really become the same. We *can,* in Christ, every one of us be this, a living stone.

i. "*A stone,*" a rock. Take the noun first. We *can,* out of whatever weakness, be *made strong* in God. Be our slightness and vacillation of character what it may, it is as possible for us as for St. Peter's converts to become stones. We can be solid, with a quiet purpose for right which "reverbs no hollowness." We can be stable, with a persistency of dutiful conduct which is utterly different, different as day from dark, from the attitude of the Pharisee, but which stays and lasts in the march of life, and is the same. You know where to find the man, you can count on him, you can be sure of him. He is steady as a rock himself, to resist and to shame temptation, and equally steady, if need be, to be leaned upon with strong reliance by a friend in moral danger. He can stand alone. He is not the poor slave of drifts and fashions of opinion and practice. Conscience and will have somehow coalesced within him, and the compound is a rock of quiet character which by no means slights popularity, but is never ruled by it for an hour.

ii. Then take the adjective. He is "a *living stone.*" He is not too good (if there be such a goodness at all) to be profoundly alive with the life of human sympathy, human insight, human affections, the life which unobtrusively cares for and is at the service of the lives around him. The living stone is no such unhappy being that he can say, that he can think, of others: "I am holier than thou." At his Lord's feet, in his Lord's holy heart, he has found an absolute corrective to such moral falsehood. Out of nature he has been taken into grace. But then by grace he has been led, if I may put it so, back into a purified *nature;* he is *natural,* with a quick readiness for every wholesome and honest sympathy; immovable in principle, unchangeable in every duty of the friend.

Such is the Christian as a living stone; a noble ideal, and, let me repeat it over again, an ideal meant to be realized, to be incarnated, in each and every one of ourselves. This man has been; this man can be.

As I speak of it, a beloved and beautiful memory rises before me—a friend of my early undergraduate days, called to die before his own degree, but first called to *live,* as a living stone. Before he entered Trinity College he had passed through a military academy, a place which at that time was a scene of deep moral pollution. Gentle and even facile as he was by nature, God, just as he entered the place, had made him "a living stone." With quiet, unshaken, unswerving steadfastness, under acutest difficulties, he *lived,* and he was a *rock.* And by the time he left the academy—I record a fact—vice was out of fashion there.

But if the stone is such, what will the structure be? Is it not a glorious thought, the possibility for good, for virtue, for all that is most Christian, when strength meets strength and life meets life in the mighty fellowship and co-operation of holy friendship, and conscious membership one of another, hand joining hand and heart joining heart in the brotherhood of the faith and of the love of Jesus Christ?

No living stone is meant to lie alone by the road. It is made what it is in order to be built with others into one, in a union of heart, of life, of work, full at once of peace and power.

This is no unfit time* to lay a solemn stress upon that thought. Sometimes the Lord's teachings are

* The sermon was preached February 4, 1900.

borne in upon us with an even awful weight by His providence. We are at a crisis in our England's life the like of which, I think, no living man has seen; for who now lives to remember the Napoleonic Wars? It is a dread time; but it is a time of sublime capacities for our highest good, and for the genuine glory of our Motherland. For it throws back each of us first upon himself and upon his God, and then binds us man to man in what can develop into an even heroic sympathy. But oh, that the sons of England may be each, in this highest sense, a living stone, and all stand together in *that* strength and life, for God and man!

Remember, as we close, that there is one secret, and only one, for the strength, the life, and the cohesion, in their inmost truth. Ultimately, that Secret is the Lord Christ, the Living Stone—Christ, in His contact, Spirit to spirit, with the man, and with the men, who come to Him. From the first, even to the last, there it must lie. The Apostle gives it to us here: Πρὸς ὃν προσερχόμενοι—"*to whom coming*"; with a coming, as the tense of the Greek participle indicates, which, though it must have a beginning, is to be then continual. Προσερχόμενοι—"coming, and coming, and coming again"; for pardon, for purity, for living power; touching

LIVING STONES. 231

(as Antæus touched his mother Earth, and was strong again), still touching, the Living Stone, that we also may be always "living stones," results of HIM.

XVI

HEART PURITY

Preached in St. Catherine's College Chapel, Cambridge

"Blessed are the pure in heart."—Matt. v. 8.

You will expect me to finish the verse, and to recite that supreme promise with which our Lord and Master crowns His benediction: "Blessed are the pure in heart, for they"—ὅτι αὐτοί they distinctively, they only—"shall see God." And I *have* now thus recited it, giving you the immortal words in full. Yes,

> "Blessed are the pure in heart,
> Who God Himself shall see;
> None may attain by other art
> That last felicity."

But on purpose to-day I have left the *promise* aside, that our thoughts may be given the more directly and the more undividedly to the wonderful benediction itself, and to just that point of infinite import in it, the testimony of Jesus Christ to the possibility of purity, to the fact that it can be said, and by His sacred lips, of a veritable human being, "He is blessed, for he is pure in heart."

HEART PURITY.

Wonderful paradox, in that Book of profound and pregnant paradoxes, the Bible. In the Bible, on the one hand, we find the human heart—not exceptional hearts, but the heart, the great abstract, realized in each individual instance—described as "deceitful above all things and desperately diseased" (for so we should render Jer. xvii. 9). The Redeemer Himself affirms* that "out of the heart of man," as from their very fount and origin, proceed "evil thoughts" and all that is impure. Yet in this same Book, upon the other hand, we read, if we will look for them, just the noblest possible utterances about the moral greatness for which man was made, and to which, out of the wreck and mire of his fall, he can again be lifted. The voice whose kind, truthful sternness tells us all we can bear to know of our evil, is the same voice which then tells us that we can be, not in dream but in fact, not hereafter only but here and now, filled with God's own pure good. We, no beings of the skies, but we ourselves, to-day, may, really may, be pure in heart.

It is something to recollect just this. If that august thing, the Christian Gospel, is the very truth (and it is either the very truth or the most complete illusion that has ever mocked the world—it is possible to be pure in heart. That simple affirmation can

* Matt. xv. 19.

be as new life itself to the man who, longing to be clean inwardly has well-nigh given up the thought, as something which must at best be relegated to an unimaginable future. Aye, and if there be a man so deeply pitiable that he has never really yet had a longing to be clean within, the quiet affirmation of the possibility may be to him, too, the first breath of life. It may generate just such a consciousness of the absolute wretchedness of inward evil as is sometimes evoked by the mere juxtaposition with it of the glory and the repose of inward good, presented as a fact, and as within the reach.

Then let us affirm it to ourselves again. There is such a thing, according to the Holy Scriptures, as heart purity; that is to say, there is such a thing as a state of the human heart, in which the man, the genuine man, the person of the present day and of modern circumstances, entirely loves the will of God, and entirely seeks to do it. There is such a thing as a human heart which, habitually, and with the joy of a steadfast sympathy, not only approves of virtue, which is conscience, but rejoices in it, as at once its liberty and its law; or rather, not in it but in Him, of whom virtue is but as the sunshine to the sun. And such joy and sympathy is purity of heart. There is such a thing as will, mind, and affection, united, not divided, against the tempter and for the will of God. There is such a thing as an internal *No* to the siren-call of evil which is entirely true, for it is but the other side of a *Yes* which "out of a pure heart fervently" responds to the call of Christ. There is such a thing, in very truth, not in legendary periods but to-day, as an unreserved choice in favor of what is wholly good; a true deliverance from that subtle and dreadful willingness to be tempted which comes of a lingering relish for the horrible pleasantness of sin; a response, not from the shifting surface of the soul, but from its depths, to the whisper of the eternal Spirit. Then it is no longer as if the will for good floated and drifted on the top, while beneath there was a deeper and a more secret will, desiring the evil after all, and as if the best that could be done was to crush down, as it were to batten down, the evil under the good, driving it only deeper in, and inevitably suggesting the thought that worse mischief is but growing and festering there for recrudescence another day. No; it can be altogether otherwise. Things can be true to virtue and to God at those "first springs of thought and will" where our true life runs up and out. The man, the real man, can take his place among the blessed ones who are pure in heart.

Do not let me be mistaken, as if I meant to say that this same man can so be and so stand as to walk out into the open, before the white light of eternal Holiness, and say: "Look at me; I have no sin." The dream, under that awful light, of an absolute sinlessness is, in itself, a moral discord, a sin, a failure to see God aright. There is for us men, to the last, no standing before the Throne but upon our perfect Redeemer's merits, no immaculate veil but His righteousness cast over us, no "way into the holiest" but along the line of His sprinkled blood.* In the noble words put by the poet into the lips of his St. Agnes, the robes indeed were white, and the flames was clear that lit the nocturnal pathway; yet

> "As these white robes are soil'd and dark
>   To yonder shining ground,
> As this pale taper's earthly spark
>   To yonder argent round;
> So shows my soul before the Lamb,
>   My spirit before Thee;
> Such in my earthly house I am
>   To that I hope to be."

No, "if we say we have no sin"—and it is the beloved Apostle who writes this "we" and "ourselves" and "us"—"we deceive ourselves, and the truth is not in us." "Enter not into judgment with Thy servant, O Lord, for in Thy sight shall no man living be justified."† The truth of heart purity will no more bear than any other great spiritual truth to

* Heb. x. 19. † 1 John i. 8, Ps. cxliii. 2.

run alone, irrespective of a balance. It is inevitable, as the whole history of Christianity tells us, and its record of dogmatic controversy in particular, that when a side of truth, however great a side, is really treated as the whole, it develops, or rather, is distorted, into an error. But that principle cuts, of course, both ways, and sometimes we have to see to it that the cautionary side of a truth does not usurp the attention due to the glorious positive to which it stands related. So it is with heart purity. If I do not mistake, men need sometimes to say to themselves words somewhat like these: "It is quite true that the subtle mystery of sin eludes my perfect comprehension. It is true, profoundly true, that till we see the Lord as He is, we shall never be fully like Him; that is, we shall never be wholly without sin. It must needs be, then, that, to the last breath, I hide myself from the eternal judgment in the "Rock of Ages, cleft for me." But then, I will not forget, I will remember with joy and hope, that, in a sense relative indeed, yet magnificently true, things can be so revolutionized in me—yea, to the depths, that my heart can be genuinely cleansed; my will can be honestly attuned to the will of God; not merely my assent, but my love, not only my moral sense, but my heart, can go out to that now beloved will. The condition of me, a sinner, can be so dealt with that the contrast with the troubled past shall be indefinitely large and bright. Heart purity, in a sense consonant with all penitent humbleness, yet a sense strong and genuine, can be mine, so that I may "walk worthy of the Lord, unto all pleasing," εἰς πᾶσαν ἀρέσκειαν,* "all meeting of His will."

Let us seek a large vision of that side of truth, that wonderful wealth of the promises of purity.

But how shall this thing be? Can I answer better than in the words of our Lord, spoken on an occasion† close to the purpose of our present thoughts? "Who then can be saved?" cried the amazed Apostles. Shall we take up their question, and give it one particular line? "Who then can be saved—from himself? Who then can be saved, deep and at the center, from the love and from the power of sin?" *"The things which are impossible with men are possible with God."*

It is a question of a miracle; the requisite is the action of none less than a Divine Person. We can, in the grace and mercy of God, put ourselves in the way of the action, even as helpless sufferers of old, the blind, the halt, the palsied, the bleeding, put themselves in the way of the Man of Nazareth. We can, in some measure, search heart and life, and really tell God about it. Within a considerable

* Col. i. 10. † Luke xviii. 26, 27.

range, we can cut ourselves off from known and preventable temptations. We can—we know it—command our eyes not to look on evil, not to trifle with the sensuous till it sinks into the sensual. We can read what God has said, in precept, warning and promise, and we can speak—the more absolutely in simplicity the better—to Him in prayer. But all these are but fences round the Secret, or avenues up to it. The Secret is the Wonder-Worker Himself, trusted, welcomed in, summoned by the soul, to be the conquering and liberating Presence in its great need, and in its depths.

We shall never do it of ourselves. At the center of things, man is powerless to be his own transfigurer; he can as soon run, he can as soon soar, from his own shadow. But his Maker and his Redeemer, as man yields himself to God, can lift him from that shadow into light, and set him free indeed. What is needed is—that PERSON, "dwelling in the heart by faith," so to make His chamber clean. "Blessed are the pure in heart." Then, "create thou in me a clean heart, O GOD."

> "Come in, O come, the door stands open now;
> I hear Thy voice; my Savior, it is Thou."

www.ingramcontent.com/pod-product-compliance
Lightning Source LLC
Chambersburg PA
CBHW060601230426
43670CB00011B/1916